Social Research Perspectives

Occasional Reports on Current Topics

14

The Risk Professionals

by Thomas Dietz and Robert W. Rycroft

George Mason
University

George Washington
University

RUSSELL SAGE FOUNDATION   NEW YORK

The Russell Sage Foundation

The Russell Sage Foundation, one of the oldest of America's general purpose foundations, was established in 1907 by Mrs. Margaret Olivia Sage for "the improvement of social and living conditions in the United States." The Foundation seeks to fulfill this mandate by fostering the development and dissemination of knowledge about the political, social, and economic problems of America. It conducts research in the social sciences and public policy, and publishes books and pamphlets that derive from this research.

The Board of Trustees is responsible for oversight and the general policies of the Foundation, while administrative direction of the program and staff is vested in the President, assisted by the officers and staff. The President bears final responsibility for the decision to publish a manuscript as a Russell Sage Foundation book. In reaching a judgment on the competence, accuracy, and objectivity of each study, the President is advised by the staff and selected expert readers. The conclusions and interpretations in Russell Sage Foundation publications are those of the authors and not of the Foundation, its Trustees, or its staff. Publication by the Foundation, therefore, does not imply endorsement of the contents of the study.

BOARD OF TRUSTEES
Gary MacDougal, Chair

Robert McCormick Adams Carl Kaysen Howard Raiffa
Anne Pitts Carter Patricia King John S. Reed
Earl F. Cheit Gardner Lindzey Madelen Talley
Philip E. Converse James G. March Eric Wanner

Library of Congress Cataloging-in-Publication Data

Dietz, Thomas.
   The risk professionals / by Thomas Dietz and Robert W. Rycroft.
    p. cm. — (Social research perspectives ; 14)
   Bibliography: p.
   ISBN 0-87154-214-5 : $6.95
   1. Environmental policy—United States. 2. Risk managers—United States. I. Rycroft, Robert W., 1945–   . II. Title. III. Series.
HC110.E5D54 1987
363.7'056'0973—dc19   87-19992
                                                                                     CIP

Copyright © 1987 by Russell Sage Foundation. All rights reserved. Printed in the United States of America. No part of this publication may be reproduced, stored in a retrieval system, or transmitted, in any form or by any means, electronic, mechanical, photocopying, recording, or otherwise, without the prior written permission of the publisher.

NOTICE of series title change: *Social Research Perspectives* is a new title for the *Social Science Frontiers* series (volumes 1–9 published 1969–1977). The numbering of *Perspectives* volumes is a continuation of the *Frontiers* numbering.

10 9 8 7 6 5 4 3 2 1

Social Research Perspectives

Occasional Reports on Current Topics from the Russell Sage Foundation

The *Social Research Perspectives* series revives a special format used by the Russell Sage Foundation for nine volumes published from 1969 to 1977 under the series title, *Social Science Frontiers*. The *Frontiers* series established itself as a valuable source of information about significant developments in the social sciences. With the re-named *Perspectives* series, we again provide a timely, flexible, and accessible outlet for the products of ongoing social research—from literature reviews to explorations of emerging issues and new methodologies; from summaries of current policy to agendas for future study and action.

The following *Frontiers* titles are still available:

5   *The Corporate Social Audit,* by Raymond A. Bauer and Dan H. Fenn, Jr. (1972)

7   *Social Forecasting Methodology: Suggestions for Research,* by Daniel P. Harrison (1976)

8   *The Vulnerable Age Phenomenon,* by Michael Inbar (1976)

9   *Work and Family in the United States: A Critical Review and Agenda for Research and Policy,* by Rosabeth Moss Kanter (1977)

Now available in the *Perspectives* series:

10   *Your Time Will Come: The Law of Age Discrimination and Mandatory Retirement,* by Lawrence M. Friedman

11   *Risk Acceptability According to the Social Sciences,* by Mary Douglas

12   *Risk Management and Political Culture: A Comparative Analysis of Science in the Policy Context,* by Sheila Jasanoff

13   *Inspectors-General: Junkyard Dog or Man's Best Friend,* by Mark H. Moore and Margaret Jane Gates

Acknowledgments

All research projects are collective efforts, drawing on the time and talents of many individuals and organizations not formally credited with authorship. This study is no exception. Our debts are substantial, and we wish to acknowledge the help of many people. First, there are the risk professionals themselves, who took time from very busy schedules to share their views with us, and who were very patient with structured interviews when they might have preferred more informal dialogue. The Russell Sage Foundation provided a grant ("The Washington Danger Establishment"), which funded the research reported here. Cynthia Boiter, Lewis Michaelson, Deborah Cornelius, Cheryl Weiner, and Sheila Barrows conducted the interviews and coded the data. Our ability to acquire high-quality data can be attributed to their skill and patience. Very special thanks go to Cindi Boiter, who worked with us for three years. Without her care and intelligence, the project would have been far less successful and far less fun. Special thanks are also due to Kim Lutz who, with Cindi, handled most of the administrative work of the project and also lent her substantial talents to coding and maintaining our sanity. Larry Regens and Paul Stern have collaborated on several aspects of this project, and we are grateful for their insights. The Center for Academic and Administrative Computing of the George Washington University and the Academic Computing Service of George Mason University were generous with computing resources. Finally, we are grateful to the Graduate Program in Science, Technology, and Public Policy of the George Washington University and the Department of Sociology and Anthropology of George Mason University for providing both intellectual and logistical support for the study.

Contents

1	Introduction	1
2	Risk Professionals as an Elite	11
3	Risk Professionals as a New Class	33
4	Risk Professionals as an Establishment	53
5	Risk Professionals as a Policy Community	77
6	Conclusions	103
Appendix A	Methodology	117
Appendix B	Interview Guide	125
Notes		145

Chapter 1 Introduction

In June 1983 William Ruckelshaus took office as the administrator of the federal Environmental Protection Agency (EPA). In the previous thirty months the agency had been a source of great controversy. The first EPA administrator in the Reagan administration, Anne Gorsuch Burford, and a number of other senior officials had resigned in the midst of allegations of unethical and illegal conduct. Ruckelshaus, a moderate Republican who had served as the first EPA head in the Nixon administration, was appointed to refurbish the agency.

The first public act of the new administrator was to deliver a speech entitled "Science, Risk, and Public Policy" to the National Academy of Sciences.[1] He did not choose a group of businessmen, environmentalists, or reporters but rather a collection of eminent scientists for his initial step in attempting to rebuild EPA's flagging credibility. And his subject was not the agency's troubles, nor his plans for the future, nor any other overtly political topic. Rather, he spoke on the use of formal risk analysis in the federal government. Why would the leader of such a troubled bureaucracy choose such a forum and subject? At first glance, it might seem as if Ruckelshaus intentionally chose an innocuous place and topic to begin his reign quietly. But in fact his presentation attracted considerable attention in the scientific, policy, and popular press. We believe that his choice of audience and theme was stark testimony to the importance of environmental risk and to the central role of science in environmental policy. In this study, we examine the relationships between science and environmental politics using environmental risk, that is, environmental threats to human health and safety, as the point of focus.

Concern about environmental threats to human health and safety is perhaps the major topic on the environmental policy agenda in the 1980s. While there are other crucial problems, concern with hazardous substances and the potential harm they do to human health and safety has dominated discussions of environmental policy for several years. Every sign indicates that this trend will increase in the future.[2] Concern with risk has produced a large number of individuals, mostly based in Washington, whose professional interests center on environmental hazards and the policy responses to these threats. In this study we examine these people and through them the role of science and politics in environmental policy.

If we ask why Ruckelshaus chose to begin his tenure by addressing the topic of risk, we should also ask why a study of risk professionals would be of interest. The general question can best be answered by responding to three more specific queries: Why environmental policy? Why the link between science and policy? And why Washington-based professionals?

Why Environmental Policy?

We believe that environmental policy issues will be among the major sources of political conflict in the next two or three decades. Analysts of all types of backgrounds and persuasions have observed that environmental policy is different than other arenas. At the most abstract level, environmental policy, especially that portion of it concerned with health and safety issues, is an area in which the state must maintain legitimacy. Whatever other functions the nation must perform, there is consensus that it must protect the public health.[3] Thus, any perceived shortfall of protection is likely to produce loud and impassioned protest from a broad spectrum of the general public, as is evident from cases such as the successful mobilization against nuclear power.[4]

Strong public interest in environmental health and safety matters would not in and of itself make the environmental policy domain interesting if the nation-state could easily respond to environmental demands using traditional policy structures and processes. But this is not the case. Environmental protection influences the production process of a society in ways that are different from most other kinds of governmental intervention. Prior to the environmental movement, most American governmental regulations were concerned with specific industries or with particular business practices. That is, until environmental issues came to the top of the national political agenda, governmental control of the private sector was fashioned after the model of economic regulatory bodies such as the Interstate Commerce Commission or the Federal Power Commission. The usual arrangement in this "old style" regulation involved the creation of a new agency with authority to monitor and intervene in the market activities of a particular industry. This regulatory/promotional role was seen as responsible for many of the alleged ills of public economic control of the private sector, such as client industry capture of regulatory bodies or bureaucratic inertia and resistance to economic or technical change. The "new style" regulation is fundamentally different. First, the new regulatory bureaucracies are broader in scope than the old-style model because they are not limited to any one industry. Their authority extends across the entire private sector. This makes it difficult for any single industry to dominate these agencies, as often happened in the traditional model. Second, and largely because of this penetration of a variety of industrial sectors, the newer federal regulators are not concerned with the totality of any company or industry but only with that portion of operations that comes under their control. This prevents them from becoming too concerned about the overall well-being of any company or industry. Instead, it may lead to "blind spots" regarding the consequences of regulation for any particular firm or sector.[5]

There are other differences. The old-style economic regulation of business often was characterized in terms of "iron triangles" composed of the regulated industry, the regulatory agency, and the congressional committees with oversight authority. The new social regulation, however, appears to be more complex. Some ob-

3

servers have argued that a new coalition of interest groups, the media, and the government itself underpins the new regulation. For example, Paul Weaver has argued that the two kinds of regulation represent "the social policy of two different classes and embody radically different political philosophies," with the new regulation the product of professionals and managers committed to "humanistic work in the not-for-profit and public sectors" and typically "hostile to the economic accomplishments and political vision of the Progressive era" during which the old regulation was developed.[6]

The Progressive reforms in America at the turn of the century mitigated the most evident problems of nineteenth-century industrial capitalism. They were followed by reforms that legitimated the labor movement and made the state increasingly responsible for social welfare. All of these policies represent compromises between the demands of labor and capital. Underpinning these compromises was the set of assumptions that have been called the "dominant social paradigm," namely, that unlimited economic growth was possible and beneficial, that most serious problems could be solved by technology, and that environmental and social problems could be mitigated by a market economy with some state intervention.[7]

Environmentalists appear to offer a "competing paradigm," which attacks many, though certainly not all, of the central values and goals of modern industrial capitalism. This alternative perspective emphasizes limits to growth, restrictions on industrial capitalism, participatory policy structures, decentralized social structures, nature's finite resources and delicate balance, and constraints on science and technology as problem solvers.[8] These views often bring environmentalists into conflict with the traditional consensus on how best to improve the human condition—the idea of progress itself.

Of course, not all supporters of policies to protect the environment adopt the new environmental paradigm that challenges assumptions underlying "politics as usual." Indeed, a number of large environmental organizations have emerged as part of the resource management and conservation movements that have been part of the development of the modern welfare state. But there seems to be substantial support for a new and challenging worldview among many environmentalists.[9] These three factors—strong public support for environmental protection, a new kind of social regulation, and an alternative worldview among environmentalists—have led to fierce battles over the last fifteen years or so.

There is no reason to believe that public concern with environmental threats to human health and safety will decline in the foreseeable future, nor is there any reason to believe that the challenge to the political and economic system presented by environmental regulation will become less profound.[10] Thus, we anticipate that environmental risk policy will continue to be an area of strenuous controversy, and that this makes it an excellent arena in which to observe the dynamics of the state and of public policy.

Why the Link Between Environmental Policy and Science?

Contemporary environmental policy is heavily intertwined with science. For the last twenty-five years research in environmental science has been uncovering the adverse impact of industrial society. While conflict may be triggered by sudden public reaction to a recent event, such as the incidents at the Three Mile Island or Chernobyl nuclear power plants, the more common experience, such as debates about nuclear fallout or the effects of acid rain, is that debates are generated in an incremental fashion by research that describes unanticipated consequences. And even in those cases where a crisis or perception of crisis dramatically alters political conflict, science serves useful functions in clarifying issues, framing judgments, and legitimizing initiatives.[11]

Environmental problems engender complex, multidimensional tradeoffs. Consider the problem of lead in gasoline. Reducing emissions of lead from automobiles will improve public health, but it also affects the chemical, gasoline, and automotive industries. In such a situation, the best policy choice is not immediately obvious, for the costs and benefits of any option are not directly commensurable, and in most instances the individuals and groups who bear the costs are not those who reap the benefits.[12] A set of techniques from the social sciences, including systems analysis, cost-benefit analysis, multiobjective optimization, and risk analysis have been applied to this kind of problem. These methods of formal policy analysis provide mechanisms for making complex tradeoffs, and are another influential application of science in the policy process. They structure policy analysis and produce results that favor one alternative over another.[13]

We are concerned with the linkage between science and policy for two reasons. First, scientific information is an important source of power in conflicts with a substantial scientific and/or technological content. Arguments about controlling the production, use, and disposal of hazardous substances are based on epidemiological and laboratory studies of the toxicity of those substances, on models of their transport and transformation, and on assessments of the costs, risks, and benefits associated with various policy choices. New data and analyses change this calculus, and only individuals with the requisite technical understanding or expertise are in a position to undertake such analyses or to critique them.[14] When individual expertise is aggregated into organizations, this power is multiplied.

Our second concern arises because environmental policy is conducted in special languages. The growth of scientific specialties in the last half of the twentieth century has made it difficult even for those with scientific training to communicate across disciplinary, or even subdisciplinary lines. Those without such training must rely on secondary accounts that translate science into popular terminology. This growth of specialization, coupled with the salience of science in policy, poses major challenges for democracy.[15] Increasingly, the ability to participate in, or even communicate about, policy debates is constrained by their degree of scientific content and the absence of mechanisms to translate science into forms that are comprehensible to the general public. This problem has become especially intense in environmental health and safety policy. These issues are highly salient to large portions of the society, but discussions are difficult to monitor for all but the most mobilized special interest groups. We hope that a better understanding of how science is used will lead to some paths along which the tension between science and democracy can be reduced.

Why Washington Risk Professionals?

If environmental risk policy provides an attractive substantive focus for analysis of political conflict and of the relationships between science and policy, then Washington is the obvious location for research. Until the 1960s this was not so evident, largely because the federal government played only a limited role in environmental policymaking. But by the end of that decade, a new movement had squarely placed environmental issues on the national policy agenda. By the middle of the 1980s, environmental protection "appeared to be a well-established function of the national government, strongly legitimated and increasingly well institutionalized."[16] Though the Reagan administration has subjected this process to a severe test, there can be no doubt that the federal government continues to be the center of environmental health and safety politics.

Just as the policy process is geographically concentrated, it is also carried out by a relatively small group of people. Division of labor in complex societies applies as much as to political as to economic processes. Mass concern about environmental issues is transformed into policy through the action of individuals who spend most of their time dealing with environmental risk concerns. We refer to them as *risk professionals*. To understand the dynamics of environmental policy, we must understand risk professionals.

Not only do the risk professionals carry out the highly diverse tasks of the risk policy system, ranging from the conducting of scientific studies to the actual implementation of policies themselves, but they are found working in all parts of that system: federal agencies, the Congress, environmental organizations, corporations. Even a slight familiarity with Washington reveals the significance of the risk professionals in shaping the way our society deals with health and safety risks.

To our surprise, we found very little empirical or theoretical literature on the risk professionals or on professionals who work in other policy systems. To be sure, there are case studies of the debate over specific risks,[17] or of the evolution of entire policy systems,[18] and assessments of one type of actor or another in a policy system.[19] But there does not seem to be a body of thought that proposes hypotheses about policy professionals nor prior studies that allow a comparison of risk professionals with those in other systems. So we have conducted a descriptive study—an ethnography or natural history of these individuals—in the hope that our work will generate a base for comparison in the future. Of course, as every ethnographer and natural historian knows, data cannot be collected, much less interpreted, in the absence of theory. We have drawn upon previous studies of the environmental movement and public opinion on environmental issues as well as on social science literature that describes how individuals and organizations are structured to influence policy.

Social scientists have developed several perspectives on the people who influence policy in complex societies. The *elite* perspective emphasizes the relationship between political power and personal background, especially wealth, education, and personal contacts.[20] A *class* perspective focuses on the links between economic interests, ideology, and efforts to influence policy. In particular, "new class" theorists have suggested that support for environmental protection comes from an emergent class whose worldviews and interests are different than those of either labor or capital.[21] Some scholars have emphasized an *establishment* within the policy process. The establishment is composed of institutionalized interests that share a common position on policy issues, such as corporations, and are distinct from challengers, such as environmental groups.[22] The *community* perspective emphasizes the linkages among actors in the policy system and the importance of regular, ongoing participation and communication.[23] Here the system is open to new members, but only to those who participate steadily and who play by the rules.

Each of these perspectives agrees that a relatively small subset of the general population engages in the policy process on a regular basis. But they differ significantly in the frameworks they offer, and as a result provide rather distinct, and sometimes incompatible, views of policymaking. We began this study in response to a comment by Thomas Schelling that a "danger establishment," parallel to the "military establishment," had emerged around issues of environmental health and safety.[24] But we have not restricted ourselves to the view that risk professionals constitute an establishment; rather, we have tried to answer questions suggested by all four major views. The perspectives are not so distinct nor so clearly articulated that we can consider them competing theories, so our goal is not to test them in any formal sense. Instead, we seek to create an integrated description of the risk policy professionals, considering their backgrounds, interests, values, and communication structures.

The Study

During 1984 we conducted interviews with 228 environmental risk professionals. We selected individuals to be interviewed based on a network sampling procedure described in greater detail in Appendix A. The interviews incorporated a set of questions derived from all the perspectives mentioned above. In Chapter 2 we consider the elite perspective and its implications. There we delineate the social, educational, and career profile of our respondents and consider the extent to which risk professionals constitute an elite.

Chapter 3 draws on the class perspective and examines the social, economic, environmental, and political ideology of our respondents. We pay particular attention to the relationship between worldview and professional training and employment in an effort to identify ideological splits among the professionals. The establishment perspective, delineated in Chapter 4, suggests that risk professionals, or at least those professionals with similar educational backgrounds and current employment, should agree on policy issues. This chapter considers our respondents' views on specific policy concerns and identifies the degree of consensus within our sample. Chapter 5 moves on to an institutional and community focus. There we analyze flows of information between individuals and organizations. The final chapter develops themes that emerged from our analysis and comments on the implications of these themes for future evaluation of environmental health and safety risk policy.

Chapter 2   Risk Professionals as an Elite

Most Americans consider the denizens of Washington a curious and alien species, to be viewed with a mixture of distrust and respect. On the one hand, Washingtonians are seen as power-hungry, self-important, and out of touch with normal life. On the other, even in the wake of Vietnam and Watergate and in the midst of "Contragate," national pride holds that we send our best daughters and sons to Washington. The mixture of contempt and respect varies over time and among individuals, but the view that those engaged in the policy process are unlike the rest of the nation is widespread, persistent, and usually accompanied by a sense that those "inside the beltway" are more less alike, an elite of "Washington types" as similar to each other as they are different from normal Americans.

Of course, the notion that those engaged in shaping state policy are distinct from the majority of those governed is not unique to contemporary America. Such views have probably been commonplace in all societies where the division of labor creates full-time political specialists. Such specialists, "those individuals who actually exercise political power in a society at any given time,"[25] are the elites of a society. The actual and proper roles of these individuals in governing society is one of the oldest themes in the social sciences. While there are many perspectives on political elites, all concur that within nation-states a relatively small fraction of the population actively engages in shaping policy, and that these individuals, by virtue of their political involvement, wield power disproportionate to their numbers.

The elite perspective emphasizes that policy specialists differ from the rest of society in social origins, personality, education, employment, and other characteristics. Some theorists argue that individuals find a place in the elite because of their exceptional intelligence, diligence, and talent.[26] Others posit that membership in the elite is determined largely by social origins, by ascribed rather than achieved characteristics.[27] Critics of the elite perspective suggest that the rate of turnover in political specialists is so high that identifying an elite is inappropriate.[28]

In this chapter we draw on the elite perspective to ask questions about the backgrounds and current circumstances of the professionals in the risk policy system. We ask, "Who are these guys?" We detail the educational histories and the gender, and the racial and generational mix of the risk professionals. We also profile their job situations, including where they work and what kind of tasks they perform, the frustrations and satisfactions they derive, and the professional affiliations that link them with professionals in other work environments.

It is no surprise that environmental health and safety policy is shaped by individuals who are not a cross-section of the American public, but in the pages that follow we go beyond the general perception that the denizens of Washington are different to a description of those differences. Most research using an elite frame of reference has focused on the highest reaches of power, the group we call the power elite. In the next section of this chapter we explicate the distinction between the power elite and the people active in the risk policy system, a policy elite. The distinction leads us to a more precise understanding of the membership of the risk policy system.

Policy Elites, Power Elites, and the Public

As noted above, most discussions of elites are concerned with power elites, or groups of individuals and institutions who wield a great deal of influence in a society, and who wield it over a variety of issues.[29] Typically, the power elite is directly involved only in the broadest aspects of policy rather than in the routine details of specific programs. They are concerned with the strategic rather than the tactical. During the last decade, sociologists and political scientists have described these individuals and institutions and have identified in some detail the links among them that appear to be critical not only for the exercise of power but also for maintaining elite solidarity and common ground for communication.[30]

In the case of environmental policy, the role of the power elite has not been studied in detail. The power elite has always been concerned with areas of exceptional beauty, and has participated in conservation schemes that were typical of the Progressive era.[31] But as noted in Chapter 1, the environmental movement of the 1960s challenged conventional business and politics and the institutions they control. This threatened the legitimacy of the power elite, and that portion of it which felt most challenged by environmentalism reacted to the threat by denying the severity of many environmental problems. The strenuous attack on Rachel Carson's *Silent Spring* is a clear example of this strategy.[32] As the environmental movement became more adept at gaining broad support, however, the existence and severity of ecological problems could no longer be denied. As a consequence, debate shifted from whether environmental regulations were needed to what kinds of controls were most appropriate.

Debate about the content and enforcement of environmental risk policy is as important as consideration of whether such policy is needed. The impact of policy on the production process or the environment depends on the exact nature of the policy and the way in which it is enforced. For example, the latitude available to agencies such as the EPA or the Food and Drug Administration (FDA) is extensive even under relatively precise mandates. Such agencies appear to be free to structure risk analysis required by statute in ways that let them have substantial control over the stringency of regulation.[33]

The shift from disputes about the place of environmental policy in the political agenda to debates about the specifics of policy has generated a new group of policy specialists whose work centers on environmental health and safety. Unlike the power elite, who deal only with broad issues, these professionals do the daily work of the risk policy system. While they have more clout than does the average citizen, the policy elite is not as influential as the power elite. And unlike the power elite, they tend to specialize, focusing their energies on a limited set of related issues. By promoting or opposing policies, by developing and interpreting data, and by administering programs they shape regulation. Their work translates popular demand for environmental protection into action.

Policy elites are an important element of any policy system. But they are of special importance in those with a high scientific and technological content. The roles of generating, translating, and using scientific information make the risk professionals more important than those involved in the day-to-day conduct of policies in domains less dependent on technical inputs.

Of course, a policy elite is not wholly distinct from either the general public or the power elite. Members of the general public who become concerned about environmental issues and become activists, or who choose careers that lead them to engage in environmental policy, may become part of a policy elite. In a parallel fashion, members of the power elite who concern themselves with policy details as well as agenda setting, with the tactical rather than the strategic, may also be part of a policy elite.

There is little research that profiles policy elites. There are a number of ethnographic studies and analyses of specific cases of policy development, as we noted in the previous chapter. And there have been a variety of excellent examinations of the power elite and their backgrounds and connections to key institutions in American society.[34] But previous research has not provided a thorough description of the actors in any policy system, that is, of any policy elite. Thus our picture of the risk elite is exploratory and we lack a basis for comparison with other systems.

Characteristics of the Risk Professionals

EDUCATION

We have argued that technical expertise is highly valued in the risk policy system. If that is the case, we would expect to find that a high proportion of the individuals working in the system will have technical training, which will be reflected in both their level of education and in the disciplines they have studied. Indeed, the educational backgrounds of our respondents are consistent with that assumption. Only 2 percent of respondents lack a college degree, only 11 percent have stopped their education with a bachelor's degree. Nearly 45 percent have doctorates. Surprisingly, for a group of policy professionals, only about 24 percent of respondents have law degrees, suggesting that while lawyers are influential in this policy system, they are not dominant. Nearly a third of the risk policy professionals have training in the physical sciences, engineering, mathematics, or statistics, with nearly one-fifth of respondents holding a doctorate in one of these fields. Only 13 percent have training in biological and environmental sciences, only 6 percent in medicine and public health. This is rather surprising for a policy domain that is centrally concerned with environmental and public health problems, and it probably reflects the prestige accorded the "hard" sciences even in policy systems that are not their natural domain. Most individuals trained in the physical and biological sciences have terminal degrees, while only about one-third of those trained in the humanities and social sciences, and about half of those trained in economics and business, possess doctorates. It appears that the generalists in the system are trained in humanities and social sciences.

The vast majority of the American power elite has been educated at a small number of elite schools, primarily Harvard, Yale, Princeton, and Stanford.[35] Elite theorists note that a common educational background, reinforced by other social ties, helps generate and maintain a common worldview on the part of the power elite. Do common educational experiences also promote homogeneity among the risk professionals? Not among our respondents. While the risk professionals are highly educated, their education is not concentrated in a few schools. Harvard, usually perceived as the most elite of American institutions of higher learning, is the most frequently attended university, accounting for 10 percent of our respondents (see Table 1). Yale and Stanford also appear with some frequency. But three Washington area schools—George Washington University, American University, and the University of Maryland—are also in the top ten institutions. Moreover, three large public schools outside the Washington area (Michigan, New York University, and Ohio State) are among the top fifteen. Thus common educational experiences do not appear to provide the kind of bond among risk professionals that they do among the power elite.

Table 1 Colleges Attended by Risk Professionals

College	Percent Attending	Number Attending
Harvard University	10.1	23
George Washington University	7.0	16
Columbia University	6.6	15
Yale University	6.6	15
University of Michigan	4.8	11
American University	4.4	10
University of Maryland	3.9	9
New York University	2.6	6
Stanford University	2.6	6
University of Virginia	2.6	6
University of Chicago	2.2	5
Cornell University	2.2	5
Duke University	2.2	5
Johns Hopkins University	2.2	5
Northwestern University	2.2	5
Ohio State University	2.2	5

GENDER AND RACE

There is a general perception that the elites of most Western societies are composed of white males. The risk professionals are no exception. Only 20 percent of our respondents are women, and only 3 percent are minorities. In addition to the gender and racial stratification that are typical of American society as a whole, environmental health and safety policy has some characteristics that may discourage participation by minorities and women. First, the importance of scientific training may be an obstacle to entry by those people who have had limited opportunities to take advantage of postgraduate education in any field, and especially low probabilities of entering advanced training in the natural and life sciences. The small number of minorities in our sample precludes a detailed examination of their educational backgrounds. But there is a strong relationship between gender and both field and level of education in our sample. While 26 percent of the men in our sample were trained in the physical sciences, mathematics, statistics, or engineering, only 13 percent of the women had such training. But women were twice as likely as men to have had training in the environmental and biological sciences. Women were three times as likely as men to have only a bachelor's degree, but only one-fourth as likely to have a law degree.

Second, there is some evidence that the press of poverty and discrimination makes environmental issues a lower priority for blacks than for whites.[36] It is reasonable that other minority groups who have suffered in this way will also emphasize social and economic issues over environmental ones. While the available analyses of race and environmentalism are for the general public, it may be that minorities entering careers in policy focus on social and economic issues, and are thus particularly unlikely to be part of the risk policy system.

In contrast, women often express greater concern for environmental problems than men. Gender differences in concern are greatest for exactly those issues that are the substantive focus of the risk policy system.[37] But women, like minorities, have been channeled out of careers in the natural sciences, so they are less likely than males to be found among an elite that focuses on technical as well as policy issues.[38] And women who have become active in environmental policy issues often opt for grassroots approaches to activism and participation, as evidenced by their role in the antinuclear and "green" movements in the United States and Europe. While the activism of social movements is critical in shaping the policy agenda, only a small proportion of such activists become members of policy elites.

AGE AND GENERATION

The political pressures that created the risk policy system were generated in large part by the "new social movements" that developed in the 1960s and 1970s. During this period, opposition to the Vietnam War raised many people's political consciousness and militancy. College-age youth were especially affected by the turbulence of this period, and played a key role in mobilizing public concern on environmental issues. Have these youth moved into the risk policy system? We found that nearly half of our sample was between 21 and 30 years of age in 1970, and thus were between 35 and 44 when interviewed. About a third of the sample was over 30 in 1970, and thus over 45 when interviewed, while 17 percent were under 21 in 1970 and thus under 35 when we interviewed them. The relative absence of people under 35 is not surprising since technical training is an important aid for involvement in the risk policy system. For example, nearly one-third of our respondents under 35 did not have graduate training. The prevalence of those aged 35–44 can be explained by the character of their college years. The politics of this period undoubtedly pushed them to consider careers that would promote the public good, and in particular careers in environmental sciences and environmental policy. The late 1960s and early 1970s were also a period during which the risk policy was developing, so there was a range of good employment opportunities in the system.

EMPLOYMENT

Where do members of the risk policy system work? What organizations are part of the system? Our sampling scheme began with individuals we were certain were a part of the system (see Appendix A), but after the first nineteen interviews, the people and organizations included in the sample were based solely on nominations from individuals already interviewed.

Given its responsibilities for managing risk and the size of the agency, it is not surprising that the largest group of our respondents (some 15 percent) are employed by the Environmental Protection Agency (see Table 2). Other executive agencies with substantial representation (between 1 and 2 percent each) include the Food and Drug Administration, the Nuclear Regulatory Commission, the Occupational Safety and Health Administration, and the Departments of Energy, Interior, and Labor and the National Science Foundation. Overall, 28 percent of the risk professionals work in executive branch agencies.

Corporations and professional and trade associations are the second largest employers, accounting for almost 17 percent of our respondents. We aggregated these two groups in the analyses that follow because the trade associations that are employers of our respondents focus their activities on the same policy issues as the corporations they represent. Since the fraction of our respondents that works for corporations and trade associations is larger than the fraction that works for EPA and about two-thirds the size of the fraction employed by the entire executive branch of

Table 2 Place of Employment of Risk Professionals, Detailed and Aggregated Categories

DETAILED CATEGORIES Organization	Percent of Sample
Environmental Protection Agency	15.4
Food and Drug Administration	1.8
Nuclear Regulatory Commission	1.8
National Institutes of Health	1.4
Occupational Safety and Health Administration	1.8
Consumer Product Safety Commission	0.4
Department of Labor	0.9
Department of Interior	1.3
Department of Agriculture	0.4
Department of Health and Human Services	0.4
Department of Energy	1.3
National Science Foundation	0.9
Other Federal Agencies	0.4
Congressional Committee Staff	6.1
Congress Member Staff	1.8
Congressional Support Organization	3.1
Consulting Firm	8.3
Law Firm	6.1
Audubon Society	0.9
National Wildlife Federation	0.4
Sierra Club	0.4
Natural Resources Defense Council	2.6
Environmental Defense Fund	1.8
Other Environmental Organizations	5.7
Regional, State, and Local Government	2.2
Labor Unions	3.9
Trade and Professional Organizations	8.7
Corporations	8.8
Universities	5.7
Think Tanks	2.2
National Academy of Sciences/National Research Council	1.3
Other	1.8

Table 2 (continued)

AGGREGATE CATEGORIES Place of Employment	Percent of Sample
Environmental Protection Agency	15.4
Other Executive Branch Agencies	12.8
Congressional Staff and Support Agencies	11.0
Law and Consulting Firms	14.4
Environmental Organizations	11.8
Corporate and Professional and Trade Associations	17.5
Think Tanks, NRC/NAS, Universities	9.2
Other (Labor, State and Local Government, etc.)	7.9
	100.0%
N = 228	

the federal government, it is clear that the private sector is highly mobilized around issues of environmental health and safety risk.

Law and consulting firms are the third largest employment category, with more than 14 percent of the risk professionals working in these organizations. Consulting firms conduct formal risk analyses and policy studies for their clients while the legal firms, which include some of the largest and most prestigious firms in the United States, are engaged in litigation and negotiation. Because information about the clients of these organizations is proprietary and sensitive, we did not ask our respondents working for law and consulting firms to provide client lists. Nevertheless, many of the risk professionals volunteered information on the type of clients for whom they typically work. From this information it appears that major corporations are the largest employers of consulting and legal firms, which is not surprising given the financial strength of these companies when compared to other participants in the risk policy system. If the proportion of the risk professionals working for law and consulting firms is added to that employed by corporations and associations, the total is about 32 percent, slightly larger than the proportion working in all federal agencies.

Eleven percent of risk professionals hold jobs in the legislative branch of the federal government. More than half of these are employed as congressional committee staff and another third work for support organizations such as the Office of Technology Assessment and the Library of Congress. As might be expected, relatively few members of the risk policy system work directly for members of Congress, since personal staff usually focus on political issues, leaving technical and policy matters to the committee staff and support arms.

Nearly 12 percent of the risk community have positions in environmental organizations. The Environmental Defense Fund (EDF) and the Natural Resources Defense Council (NRDC) are the most prominent environmental groups in the risk policy system, together accounting for over a third of employees of such organizations in the system. No more than 1 percent of our respondents were employed by any other environmental organization. Most of these groups are concerned with environmental health and safety risks, but do not have as many staff working on these issues as EDF and NRDC.[39]

University faculty who do research on risk issues compose about another 6 percent of the risk policy system. Staff at private think tanks account for an additional 2 percent, while the National Academy of Science/National Research Council employs 1 percent or so. Altogether, employees of independent research groups, think tanks, and the like constitute about 9 percent of our respondents.

State, local, and regional governments are not heavily represented. We believe this is because visibility in the risk system requires a degree of technical specialization or issue specialization. State, local, and regional government officials are unlikely to develop in these directions. Instead, they tend to work in several different policy systems, turning to consultants and federal agencies when special expertise is required.

Labor unions account for about 4 percent of our sample. American labor unions, especially the United Autoworkers and the United Steelworkers, have long been supportive of environmental protection, even when corporations have attempted to argue a "jobs versus environment" position. And unions are quite concerned with the policies of the Occupational Safety and Health Administration (OSHA), which is an important, though not central, part of the environmental risk policy system. But despite a common perception of bloated union bureaucracies hovering in the halls of Congress and regulatory agencies, we find that the participation of labor in the risk system is limited to the efforts of a small number of Washington staff who focus their concern on risk.

Washington is known as a city of transients. Each election brings new officials and also signals a shuffling of jobs by many unelected actors in the policy system. How long do members of the risk policy system stay in their jobs? Environmental organizations are dependent on public contributions and grants for their survival, and they provide fewer tangible rewards than other organizations, so we might expect them to have the highest turnover rates, as staff "burn out" from hard work, low perquisites, and formidable opponents. Conventional wisdom also suggests there is low turnover in government positions, where bureaucratic lethargy is thought to prevail. The rate of attrition in the private sector is expected to be relatively high, as presumed corporate efficiency generates rapid change.

The data from our survey belie these notions (see Figure 1). There is very little difference between the job longevity of individuals employed by environmental groups and those working in the federal government. And individuals employed by the private sec-

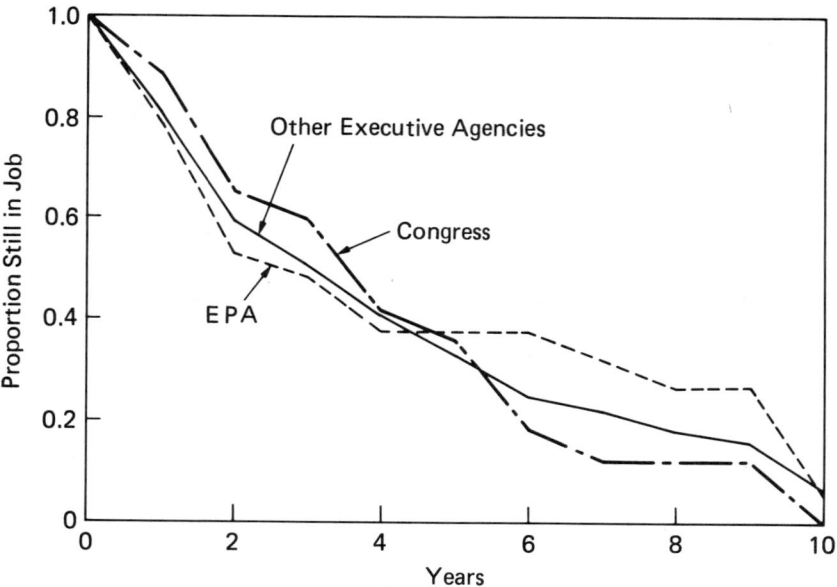

Figure 1   Job Duration of Risk Professionals, by Employer

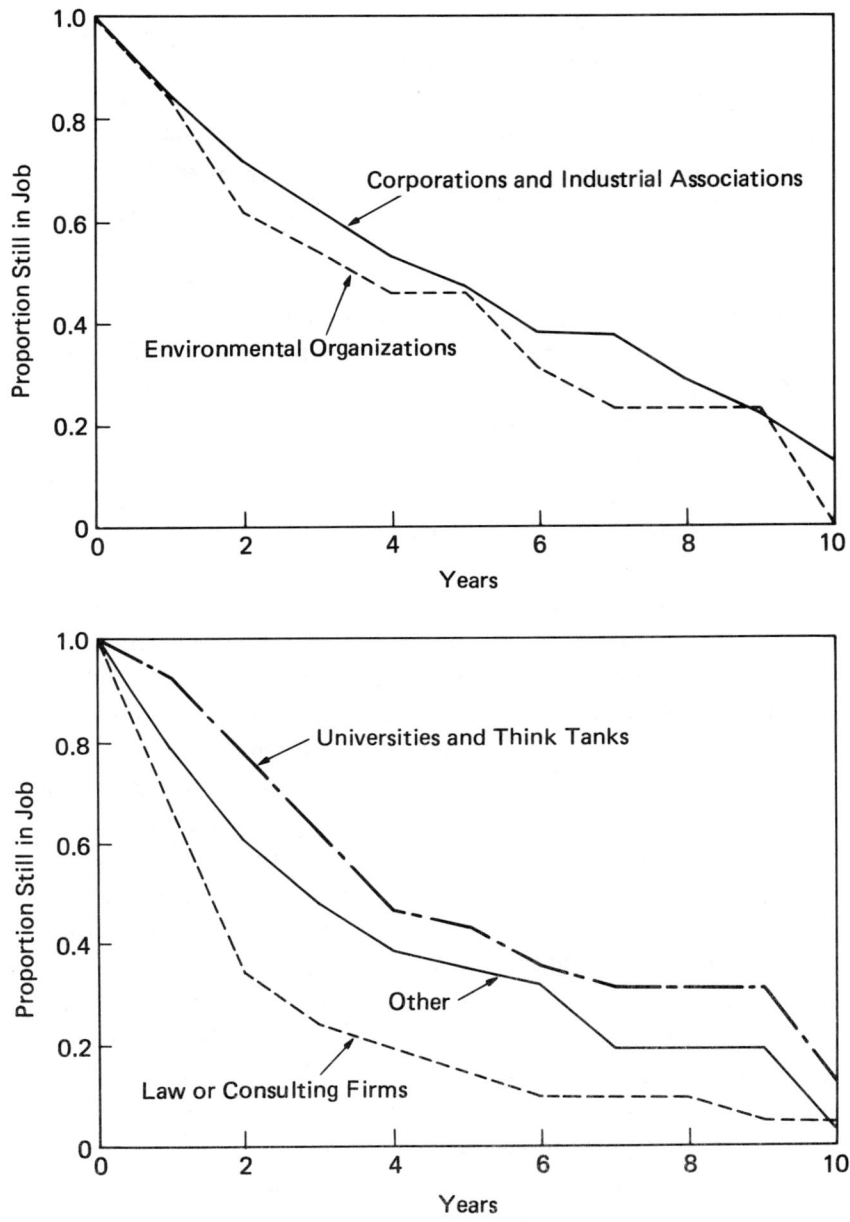

Figure 1, continued

tor are the most likely to stay on the job for long periods of time. The government turnover rate may be due to lowered morale among public sector workers dealing with environmental issues during the Reagan administration.[40] On the other hand, the longevity of corporate employment could be attributed to high pay, good perquisites, and corporate bureaucracies that are no more efficient than other large organizations. One interesting result is the high job turnover among employees of law and consulting firms. In some sense, this is the "free market" of the risk policy system. These organizations are continually seeking clients and contracts. Individuals who are successful in this enterprise are tempted to start their own business or move on to a new firm that provides better opportunities. And people who are not successful are not rewarded and must find new employment. Thus, there is little reason to expect longevity in these kinds of positions.

There is a strong relationship between place of employment and education among the risk professionals. About one-third of EPA and other federal employees in our sample, and a slightly higher proportion of those at think tanks and universities, have graduate degrees in the physical sciences, engineering, mathematics, or statistics. Only 8 percent of environmental organization employees have such training. At other places of employment, the proportion of physical scientists is between one-sixth and one-quarter. Two-fifths of environmental organization employees have law degrees, compared with one-third of congressional employees, one-fifth of those working in federal agencies other than the EPA, one-fifth of corporate and trade association employees, and one-tenth of EPA employees. Nearly one-quarter of environmental organization employees have graduate degrees in the social sciences and humanities, while at EPA and other federal agencies less than 10 percent of our respondents had graduate training in these fields. The general pattern seems to be that environmental groups do not rely on internal technical expertise, which is not surprising given their limited resources.[41] Instead, the members of the risk system working in environmental organizations are either generalists or attorneys who use research information generated elsewhere to support their arguments. As we demonstrate in the next section, this is entirely consistent with the information we have on the nature of the tasks performed by the risk professionals across the wide variety of work settings.

The Work

What kinds of work do our respondents do, and how do they feel about it? It is rather difficult to classify the many types of work that takes place within a policy system. We have divided these responsibilities into four broad categories: research, including both its conduct and supervision; translating research into policy and communicating its implications to others; work on policy per se, including lobbying and litigation; and other kinds of tasks, including education and management. Each respondent could choose several categories, so that, for example, an individual might be involved in both research and in its translation.

About half our respondents work directly on policy, 40 percent translate research into policy, and slightly more than one-quarter are engaged in the conduct and supervision of research (see Table 3). There are sharp differences in work activities across or-

Table 3 Type of Work of Risk Professionals (Percent)

Place of Employment	Research	Translating Research into Policy	Policy	Other
Environmental Protection Agency	18.9	58.8	35.3	5.9
Other Executive Branch Agencies	34.5	55.2	27.6	13.8
Congress	28.0	32.0	64.0	0.0
Environmental Organizations	14.8	25.9	74.1	22.2
Consulting and Law Firms	42.4	27.3	39.4	24.2
Corporations and Trade Associations	18.4	42.1	57.9	10.5
Universities and Think Tanks	71.4	19.0	4.8	23.8
State and Local Governments, Labor, etc.	5.3	47.4	57.9	21.0
Percentage of All Respondents	28.8	39.4	45.6	14.6

$N = 226$

ganizations. Only in think tanks and universities do a majority of risk professionals indicate their involvement in research. In the executive branch of the federal government, a majority have some involvement in the translation of research into policy, while in all other organizations the majority of respondents work directly on policy.

The contrast between environmental organizations and corporations and trade associations is interesting. Both groups report little research involvement, and policy work is the relevant activity in both cases. But fewer than one-quarter of the respondents based in environmental organizations report responsibilities at the intersection of science and policy, while over 40 percent of corporate employees report such responsibilities. This is consistent with our analysis of education by employer. Environmental organizations have constrained resources and cannot engage in much original research. It appears that they derive technical information from secondary sources rather than conducting their own analyses or interpreting the secondary literature. In contrast, corporations and trade associations have internal technical staff as well as the resources to take advantage of external consulting expertise.

We asked our respondents to identify the biggest frustrations and greatest satisfactions associated with their jobs. There was substantial consensus that the greatest satisfactions had to do with having an impact on policy (the response of about two-thirds of the risk professionals) or the basic character of the work itself, knowing they have done a good job, and other intrinsic factors (identified by half the respondents). About one-sixth of our sample focused on extrinsic rewards, such as salary and prestige, and one in ten found satisfaction in informing the public or doing research.

Frustrations were harder to categorize. The most common responses centered on a lack of resources, including time, money, and staff. Some 20 percent of the risk professionals mentioned frustration with the bureaucracy involved in the environmental policy process, the complicated and antagonistic politics of the process, or the difficult and intractable character of the conflicts that arise in risk policy.

Professional Affiliations

As we noted above, the individuals who work in the risk policy system are professionals in the area of risk policy, by definition. But many of them are also professionals in traditional scientific disciplines, in law or medicine, or in newly emerging disciplines and specialties. Since expertise is a major source of influence within the risk policy system and expertise is validated in part by professional association membership, we expected a large portion of our respondents to be affiliated with professional associations. We found this to be the case. Our respondents exhibit a substantial diversity of such memberships. Not surprisingly, the "lower house" of the American scientific community, the American Association for the Advancement of Science, is the most common affiliation, with over one-fifth of our respondents claiming membership (see Table 4). But it is something of a surprise that almost as many do not belong to any professional association. This is significant because of the role professional bodies play in maintaining an autonomous identity for people with similar professional socialization, even when they are located in disparate organizations, each with its own internal ideology. Professional association membership may also provide important communications linkages between people and the organization for which they work. But this pattern does not seem to hold with members of the risk policy system. Less than 15 percent of our respondents reported membership in the Society for Risk Analysis, the newly founded organization that focuses precisely on the kinds of issues of concern in the risk policy system. The attorneys among our respondents are members of various bar associations, especially the American Bar Association and the District of Columbia Bar Association. Other professional bodies seem to be attractive because of specific disciplinary training or interest, such as the American Chemical Society, the Society for Toxicology, the American Statistical Association, and the American Psychological Association, all of which appear with some frequency. Two bodies that have a broad, rather than disciplinary scientific membership were also cited frequently: Sigma Xi, the national science honorary society, and the New York Academy of Sciences, which has sponsored a number of symposia on policy issues. But while 80 percent of our respondents listed some professional memberships, and

Table 4 Professional Organization Memberships of Risk Professionals

Organization	Percent	Number
American Association for the Advancement of Science	23.6	53
Society for Risk Analysis	14.2	32
American Bar Association	12.0	27
District of Columbia Bar Association	9.8	22
California Bar Association	1.3	3
Other Bar Associations	8.8	20
American Chemical Society	8.4	19
Sigma Xi	6.2	14
New York Academy of Sciences	5.8	13
Society for Toxicology	5.8	13
American Economics Association	5.3	12
American College of Toxicology	4.9	11
American Public Health Association	4.0	9
Society for Occupational and Environmental Health	4.0	9
American Physical Society	3.6	8
American Statistical Association	3.1	7
Air Pollution Control Association	2.7	6
American Industrial Health Association	2.7	6
American Psychological Association	2.2	5
No Professional Memberships	18.2	41
Other	92.4	208

$N = 225$

many identified multiple ones, the organizations are so diverse that none serves as common ground for the risk professionals. We suspect that Washington itself is the common ground, as the high levels of interorganizational job mobility (described in Chapter 5) indicates. It may be that Amitai Etzioni is correct when he asserts that there now exists a great "Washington Metropolitan University" incorporating not only the traditional academic institutions but also the host of think tanks, government research centers, foundations, and the like, replete with seminars and formal and informal gatherings.[42] If so, it may well serve our respondents in the same way that traditional associations serve professionals who are not part of a policy system.

Conclusion

What have we learned by looking at the risk professionals as a policy elite? The elite perspective suggests that actors in the policy system will share common gender, ethnicity, and educational background. This homogeneity in background will be reinforced by common links in employment, work, and ties external to work, such as professional association membership. The common background and affiliations of an elite in turn create a basis for solidarity, sustain a worldview, and help to differentiate the elite from the general population.

The risk professionals have only a few of the characteristics suggested by the elite perspective. Like most Western elites, they are predominantly white males. But while most members of the risk policy system are highly educated, there is great diversity in the fields studied by the risk professionals and in the universities they attended. "Old school ties" do not form a basis for solidarity among the risk professionals, nor do the fields of education or professional association memberships suggest a common ground based on discipline. Further, the risk professionals are not concentrated in a few organizations or types of organizations. Rather, we find them employed in dozens of agencies, firms, and groups. Indeed, none of our eight major organizational groups (EPA, other federal agencies, congressional staff and support agencies, law and consulting firms, environmental organizations, corporations and trade associations, think tanks and universities, and other) serves as a home for more than 18 percent of our respondents.

Because of their influence on environmental risk policy, the risk professionals, by definition, are a policy elite. But they do not share the common backgrounds and organizational links that have been shown to create solidarity in the power elite and that we suspect operate in many other policy systems. Instead we find great diversity. Since the risk policy system lacks the solidarity that might result if members of the system shared a common background, it is no surprise that the risk policy system remains very conflictual and continues to reflect the strong conflicts over environmental risk policy that we discussed in Chapter 1. Even if the issues debated are large and contentious, common backgrounds and ties may create solidarity among the participants in a policy system and may facilitate "professional" debate and compromise. We suspect that this is true in many policy systems. However, if there is common ground among the members of the risk policy system, it is not based on the solidarity of common ties. In the next three chapters we will use "new class," establishment, and community perspectives to examine other sources of solidarity and diversity within the risk policy system. But first we consider some implications of these results for the role of science in the policy system.

The diversity we have seen in the risk policy system is highly structured. There are strong, systematic associations between where our respondents work, their educational backgrounds, and the kinds of work they do. In particular, environmental organizations are noticeably different from the rest of the system in that they are less likely to employ individuals with graduate degrees in the natural sciences, are more likely to employ attorneys, and have relatively few staff whose major job activities involve research. We believe these differences between environmental organizations and the rest of the policy system are a consequence of the resource constraints faced by the environmentalists. Environmental organizations operate with budgets that are a fraction of the financial resources commanded by even the smallest federal agency active in the policy system. The budgets are typically much smaller than funding levels available to the corporate offices and trade associations engaged in the system. Since research is an expensive and time-consuming process, environmental organizations cannot undertake it and must depend instead on information generated by others, especially think tanks, universities, and the federal government. On the other hand, environmental groups employ attorneys who can litigate and negotiate for the organization at a fraction of the cost that would be required to hire lawyers from most Washington legal firms involved in the risk policy system.

The distribution of resources, and thus of scientific expertise, has important implications for the functioning of the risk policy system. As we noted in Chapter 1, risk policy is driven in part by environmental science. But the scientific aspects of risk policy are fraught with uncertainty. Experts disagree on nearly every significant issue debated within the system. The scientific dependence of environmental organizations, and especially the fact that most research is funded by either corporations or government, leads to a certain skepticism about these analyses on the part of environmentalists. For this reason, we would expect environmental groups to reject too much reliance on science within the policy system. This hypothesis is examined in the next two chapters, in which we also explore other perspectives on the risk policy system.

Chapter 3   Risk Professionals as a New Class

Radical environmentalists and radical antienvironmentalists have highly critical views of those engaged in the environmental policy process. Antienvironmentalists such as former Interior Secretary James Watt seem convinced that Washington is a den of subversive "greens" who, with the support of liberal intellectuals, are attempting to ruin American society. In contrast, David Foreman, founder of Earth First!, has warned that professional environmentalists may have "a higher loyalty to the political process than to conservation" and have lost sight of the core values of environmentalism.[43] In this chapter we explore the worldview of the risk professionals, and examine the degree to which they adopt the views of the environmental movement and of the new class.

As we noted in Chapter 1, several students of the new social regulation and of the environmental movement have suggested that the impetus for regulation has come from a new class. While the idea of an emerging new class has great appeal to writers across the political spectrum, there is no consensus on the definition of this class. Thus, before we can use the new class perspective we must outline its essential characteristics and how they relate to the worldview of the environmental movement and the values and attitudes of our respondents.

The New Class, the Environmental Movement, and Risk Professionals

During the last three to four decades, there has been a substantial increase in the number and percentage of the population of industrialized countries who are well educated and who hold professional jobs. The position of these individuals is rather different than that of either labor or capital, and there has been a great deal of speculation that they have values and interests quite different from those of the "old" classes, labor and capital. While there are many ways of defining the new class, we believe the key criteria are education, professional employment, and employment outside the capitalist sector of the economy.[44] The rationale for education as an indicator of new class status is that college trains students in a worldview that emphasizes critical thinking and open debates, while deemphasizing material values. This in turn makes the college-educated more critical of the fundamental assumptions of society, and more willing to entertain alternative worldviews that are justified through open discussion.[45] The requirement for a professional position is closely related to this educational dimension. Professionals have the opportunity to make use of the rational, critical analysis learned as part of their education, and thus continue in work that is more or less intellectual in nature.[46] Employment outside the capitalist sector of the economy is a requisite for new class membership because those working in professional and managerial positions in the private sector are subject to the discipline of profitability, and thus less likely to develop values that oppose a competitive, growth-oriented social system. In contrast, those working in the public sector do not face this obstacle to the development of a critical worldview. It should be noted, however, that few theorists have made employment in the public sector an absolute requirement for membership in the new class.[47]

Taken together, these are useful guidelines for defining new class membership. But they do not quite fit our respondents. As we observed in Chapter 2, the risk professionals are so highly educated that almost all of them fit that criterion of the definition, and all of them are carrying out professional work. The distinction between public and private sector employment also tells us little when we consider activists in a policy system. An individual who works for an industry association may be part of the not-for-profit sector of the economy, but he or she cannot be expected to eschew the values of the corporations that are members of that association. About 76 percent of our respondents work outside the capitalist sector of the economy, but a large portion of this group work for organizations that are closely linked to that sector. In this context, there is no way to separate those organizations that are in the capitalist sector of the economy from those that are not.

Something else is needed, and we believe it is provided by the environmental movement itself. In Chapter 1 we noted that environmentalism offers a strong challenge to the dominant worldview of the industrial societies. The new class would be a logical place to find support for such a worldview. The education and professional employment of new class members provide a fertile ground for development of the new environmental paradigm as a challenge to the dominant social paradigm. And employment outside the capitalist sector of the economy would make it easier to accept challenges to the propriety of growth, profit, and private decisions about the allocation of scarce resources.

Stephen Cotgrove goes so far as to define the new class in terms of an environmentalist worldview. He says:

> Environmentalists are drawn predominantly from a specific fraction of the middle class whose interests and values diverge markedly from other groups in industrial societies. To define class in terms of some objective criteria such as relation to the means of production, or function, runs the danger of imposing categories which fail to mesh with the consciousness and behavior of groups of individuals. But if we anchor our discussion in the observable behaviors and utterances of identifiable groups, then there is a strong case for arguing for the emergence of a new class from the 1960s onwards. The growth of a new radicalism among social workers, teachers, lawyers, and psychiatrists, sharpened the antagonism between those closely tied to production functions as managers, technologists and scientists, and those in the non-productive welfare and creative occupations. It is the same constituency which supported the radical environmentalist movement.[48]

We believe that the grouping of class, ideology, and social movement into a single variable ignores distinctions that are valuable in studies of society as a whole. But we concur that the new class adopts the worldview of the environmental movement. The complexities of defining class membership for participants in a policy system precludes asking questions about class per se, but the new class perspective leads us to questions about the worldviews of risk professionals. In particular, do members of the risk policy system hold environmentalist/new class values? Before we answer that question, we must discuss the nature of those attitudes and values in more detail.

Environmentalism: Two Competing Paradigms

For some time, observers of environmental issues in the Western democracies have argued that two competing paradigms have emerged from the debates about these issues. These paradigms constitute ideologies which individuals use to structure and interpret their world. The older of the two, typically termed the dominant Western worldview or the dominant social paradigm, represents what appears to have been the consensus view of both left and right in the post-World War II period. It incorporates a belief in market mechanisms, technological optimism and the assumption that humans are and should exercise increasing control over nature. In contrast, the new environmental paradigm has emerged in response to a growing awareness of serious environmental problems and resource shortages. The new environmental paradigm is critical of the assumptions underlying the dominant paradigm and offers an alternative view of the world.[49] This paradigm may form a common ground for discussion within the risk policy system, a set of core values that can frame debates.

Stephen Cotgrove and Andrew Duff have provided a framework that can be used to contrast the new environmental paradigm with the dominant social paradigm in a fashion that allows us to develop questions about specific attitudes.[50] We have adopted their approach with some modifications. In examining the values of the risk professionals, we focus on four thematic areas across which the two paradigms appear to differ sharply. The first of these is the capitalist *economy*, where the environmental paradigm doubts the ability of the market mechanism to protect the environment and questions the benefits of economic growth and material consumption. In contrast, faith in the market and advocacy of growth and consumption are at the core of the dominant social paradigm. Second, there are differences with regard to the *polity*. The environmental paradigm believes in participation, is critical of the current political process, and tends to view the state as the potential, if not the actual, counterbalance to corporate power. The dominant social paradigm, on the other hand, supports the status quo, is more critical of citizen involvement, and sees great benefit in a cooperative link between government and business. Third, at the core of the new environmental paradigm are beliefs about the relationships between humans and *nature*. The environmental paradigm is highly critical of the impact of modern technology on the environment and sees humans as the source of major environmental disruption, while the traditional paradigm looks upon technological progress positively and is less concerned about scientific and technical *knowledge*. The environmental paradigm doubts that environmental problems can be reduced to technical matters, sees science as inexplicably intertwined with politics but also tends to favor government planning. The dominant paradigm holds that science is neutral and that increased scientific knowledge can lead to the resolution of technical problems, but tends to be more critical of government planning. Of course these dimensions are strongly interrelated, and we delineate separate dimensions as a mechanism to organize responses to specific questions, not in an attempt to argue that they are distinct.

Here we note that we are indebted to previous work for a number of questions used in this and the next chapter.[51] In the discussion that follows we note those items for which we are able to compare our results with prior analyses. In addition, several items on the "nature" dimension were drawn from the "new environmental paradigm" scale developed by Riley Dunlap and Kent Van Liere.[52]

ECONOMY

As noted above, theory suggests a major divergence between the two competing paradigms on questions of reliance on market forces. For our purposes, the key issues have to do with whether these forces, carried out through the private sector, reduce the risks to which people are exposed, or whether some form of public intervention is a better guarantee of public safety.

We asked our respondents to respond to the following four statements:

1. Development of advanced technology should continue in as uninhibited a regulatory environment as reasonably possible.
2. The benefits of modern consumer products are more important than the pollution caused by their production and use.
3. A consumer should be allowed to choose between a very safe product at a higher price and the same product without safety equipment at a lower price.
4. On the whole business does a good job of protecting the public from dangerous products and substances.

On all four questions there is broad pro-environment support among the risk professionals. When "strongly agree" and "agree" response categories are combined, and the same is done for "disagree" and "strongly disagree," we find that majorities reject the notions that advanced technology should continue in a reasonably uninhibited regulatory environment (55.7 percent), that benefits of modern consumer products are more important than their pollution (59.5 percent), that consumers should be allowed to choose between a very safe product at a higher price and the same product at a lower price without safety equipment (60.5 percent), and that business does a good job in protecting the public from hazards of production (50.9 percent).

The response to business performance in protecting the public can be compared to two studies, the first of which is a Louis Harris study of a sample of government officials (forty-seven commissioners of federal regulatory agencies) and corporate officials (402 members of executive committees of the 1,506 largest public and private corporations in the United States) as well as a sample of the general public. And the issue of consumer choice of products is comparable to both the Harris study and an analysis by Frances Lynn, consisting of interviews with 136 specialists in occupational safety and health, drawn from industry, academia, and government.[53] On the question of business performance, our respondents are much more negative than Harris's general public (about two-thirds of whom agreed that business was doing a good job) and about the same as the sample of federal regulators (some 49 percent of whom disagreed). Perhaps more striking, our respondents are much more critical than either the general public or the federal regulators on the question of consumer choice of products. Fully 51 percent of both Harris's general public and federal regulators agreed with this idea. Lynn's occupational health and safety specialists are much closer to our respondents on this item. Majorities in all three of her categories (industry, government, and academia) disagreed with the statement. Even among her industry sample, only 36 percent supported the idea. In other words, across both environmental and occupational health and safety fields, it appears as if the majority of professionals do not believe that consumer choice is sufficient to protect the public safety. As Lynn notes, this is an implicit rejection of the 1983 suggestion made by James Miller III, then head of the Federal Trade Commission and currently director of the Office of Management and Budget, that "imperfect products should be available because consumers have different preferences for defect avoidance."[54]

POLITY

The second major dimension of environmentalism focuses upon the degree to which individuals believe the polity is more representative of the public interest, as opposed to more narrow, special interests. Again, we presented four statements to our respondents:

1. A high level of public involvement often leads to bad policy decisions.
2. The political process treats most groups fairly.
3. Most policy decisions reflect the needs of special interest groups rather than the needs of the general public.
4. In our democratic society it is healthy to have an adversary relationship between business and government in areas such as product safety, pollution standards, and safety in the workplace.

At its root, this dimension attempts to tap the level of support for more participatory sociopolitical structures that are less hierarchical and that are more prone to respond to distributional concerns than the classic efficiency orientation of the dominant social paradigm.

On each of the statements sizable majorities responded according to environmentalist positions. In fact, the *lowest* level of support was almost 60 percent, on the statement about public–private adversarial relationships. On the other three issues, between 60.9 and 79.8 percent were in support of the environmental worldview. For people involved in national policy, this is striking. Members of the risk profession clearly are not threatened by citizen involvement in environmental affairs, and they express strong cynicism about the public interest orientation of current policy.

NATURE

Attitudes about nature lie at the heart of every attempt to define the new environmental paradigm. To tap this dimension, we posed four statements to the risk professionals:

1. The balance of nature is delicate and easily upset by human activities.
2. Humanity is severely abusing the environment.
3. Society has perceived only the tip of the iceberg with regard to the risks associated with modern technology.
4. The risks associated with advanced technology have been greatly exaggerated by events such as Three Mile Island or Love Canal.

Again, we found majorities in support of the alternative paradigm. The smallest of these majorities came on the statement addressing the exaggeration of risks of advanced technology, and even then some 54 percent disagreed with the position. Highly emotional and controversial examples (Three Mile Island and Love Canal) were invoked to measure strength of this position in extreme cases. On each of the other statements, majorities of between 63.7 and 69.1 percent were found in support of the alternative view.

This set of attitudes appears to be a marked departure from the technological optimism and control of nature perspective of the dominant paradigm. Instead, risk professionals stress the delicacy of ecological balance, the high magnitude of technological hazards, and the heavy burden placed on the environment by human activities. The degree to which these people are proenvironment on the nature dimension is even more dramatic when compared with the work of Harris and Lynn.

We are able to make such a comparison on two of these statements. Regarding whether society has perceived only the tip of the iceberg of modern technological risks, our respondents' 63.7 percent agreement compared to 62 percent agreement for Harris's general public and only 38 percent for federal regulators. Similarly, on the issue of Three Mile Island and Love Canal's exaggerated risks, the risk professionals' 54 percent disagreement compares to the federal regulators' 49 percent disagreement and 40 percent for the general public in the Harris study.

In the study by Lynn, the occupational health and safety experts were more inclined to believe that the risks of technology have been exaggerated than were our respondents (fully 82 percent of industry representatives agreed with the statement, and almost half of the other respondents did so). Lynn's government and university representatives, however, were more inclined than the risk professionals to say that we have seen only the tip of the iceberg with regard to risks (68 percent of each group responding positively).

KNOWLEDGE

The final dimension of environmentalism concerns the individual's confidence in science and technology, the utility of technical information, and the linkages between understanding of risks and social policy.

As with each of the other dimensions, we asked respondents to react to four statements:

1. Scientific information is often used to justify decisions made on political grounds.
2. Many environmental policy problems could be resolved with better technical information.
3. No substance should be permitted to be added to any food or drug if it is found to induce cancer when consumed in any dosage by humans or animals.
4. The government should engage in more long-range planning.

An overwhelming majority of the risk professionals support the argument that science is often used to justify political decisions, and a similar finding emerges from the statement that many issues could be resolved with better technical information (81 percent in agreement). On the surface, these two positions appear to be in conflict. After all, if science is often a device for legitimization, why the optimism about resolving problems with better technical data? Indeed, we include agreement with the technical-information-as-problem-solver statement as supportive of the old dominant social paradigm. But a word of caution must be injected here. From an environmentalist point of view, there may be no conflict at all in this pattern of responses. At least part of the explanation, outlined in some detail in Chapter 4, may have to do with the risk professionals' views of the inadequacy of data and analysis capabilities at present. If existing data and means of extrapolation are weak, then it is possible to be extremely skeptical of the use of scientific information today while still remaining optimistic about the development of a better and more broadly based scientific capability in the future.

This point is underlined by the response to our fourth knowledge statement, which raises the issue of whether government should engage in more long-range planning. More than 87 percent of the respondents agree with this statement. Thus, while there is very limited confidence in the utility of science, there is a positive response to the notion that government should move beyond the current short-term focus to more anticipatory policy strategies and mechanisms.

Our final knowledge-oriented statement elicits attitudes that appear to support the dominant social paradigm. When asked about a zero-risk approach to controlling carcinogens in the food chain, our respondents are highly negative. Almost 71 percent disagree with this line of thought. Again, at first glance, this is a marked departure from the relatively consistent pattern of proenvironmentalist positions taken on other items. But zero-risk (Delaney Clause) strategies have been in disrepute for some time in our policy system, because the techniques for detecting and measuring hazards have improved so dramatically. It may well be that our respondents concur with the position taken by many observers that alternative risk-reduction strategies are more realistic and effective than attempting to eliminate all threats.[55]

In sum, we find little support for the dominant social paradigm among risk professionals. To the contrary, strong support appears to exist for the competing environmental outlook on all four of our dimensions. Even when treating the two responses to knowledge questions as supportive of the old dominant worldview, each of the four dimensions still has, on the average, more than half the total responses supporting the environmental point of view. Moreover, there is strong, unambiguous support for the new paradigm on two of our dimensions—the polity and nature components. On balance, the majority of our respondents appear to have, in the words of Cotgrove and Duff, "different beliefs about nature and man's relations with his environment, about how the economy can best be organized, about politics and about the nature of society."[56]

Sources of Variation in Environmentalism

In the general population, environmental attitudes are systematically linked to other characteristics of individuals. Women, young people, and the well-educated tend to be more supportive of the new environmental paradigm than other segments of the population.[57] Among risk professionals we should also expect systematic variation in support for environmentalism. As in the general population, we would anticipate that age and gender may influence attitudes among those who work in the risk policy system. On the other hand, we would not expect level of education to be an important determinant of worldview for risk professionals, since it varies only slightly among this group. But field of education may be important. Alvin Gouldner distinguishes "technical intelligentsia whose intellectual interests are primarily technical" from "intellectuals whose interests are primarily critical, hermeneutic and hence often political." The former are likely to be trained in the physical sciences or in economics, while the latter are usually trained in the social sciences or humanities. Gouldner suggests that these two segments of the new class can differ markedly in their positions and worldview.[58] We hypothesize that among the risk professionals field of education will have a substantial influence on environmentalism, with those educated in humanities, social sciences, ecology, and biology most supportive of the new environmental paradigm.

Place of employment also should have a major effect on environmentalism. By our definition, those working for corporations are not part of the new class and should have limited sympathy for new class values, while environmental group employees should be staunch proponents of the new environmental worldview. Where other members of the risk policy system should stand is less clear. Environmentalists and antienvironmentalists alike often accuse government officials of siding with their opponents.

Finally, because environmental issues are usually considered liberal concerns, we examine the relationship between political ideology and environmentalism.

AGE/COHORT

In Chapter 2 we noted the relative paucity of younger members of the risk profession, but we also observed that more than half of our respondents were young adults during the 1960s and early 1970s, a key period in environmental issue formulation and policy development. Thus, either a maturation or cohort explanation might account for whatever relationship exists between the age of our respondents and their support for an environmentalist paradigm.[59]

The results of our analysis indicate that age is linked to the new worldview on some elements of our four dimensions of environmentalism, with the strongest relationship on the nature dimension. Our younger respondents are strongly supportive of an environmentalist position on the issues regarding whether society has seen only the tip of the iceberg regarding technological risks and whether the risks of technology are exaggerated. Younger (under 35) members of the risk profession also tend to be more supportive of a zero-risk standard for carcinogens in the food chain, and they are more likely to reject the argument that business does a good job in protecting us from hazards.

GENDER

As was the case with age, gender is most clearly linked to the nature dimension of environmentalism. In fact, there is a pattern of relationships between gender of respondent and views of threats to the natural environment that dramatically parallels the age pattern. Each of the three nature-related items to which age was linked in a significant fashion is also related to gender. Our women respondents, to a significantly greater extent than the men, feel that the balance of nature is delicate and easily threatened by humans, that we are seeing only the tip of the iceberg with regard to these threats, and that the risks of modern technology have not been exaggerated. Gender also is related to the economic issue of whether business does a good job of protecting the public from hazards. The female respondents do not believe it does (only 30.3 percent agreed, compared to 53.6 percent for men). And on another economic item, the females do not believe the benefits of production exceed pollution (a startling 88.2 percent disagreed with this statement).

FIELD OF EDUCATION

To our surprise, the field of education of risk professionals has little apparent relationship to attitudes and values. As we expected, our data give no indication of a relationship between level of education and environmentalism. Whether our respondents have a bachelor's degree or less or a graduate degree in medicine, science, or engineering does not seem to matter. And on the more complex issue of education *field* we find the same lack of pattern. We anticipated some relationship between a respondent's education field and the knowledge dimension of the new worldview. But on these four items, there are no great differences between the responses of lawyers, who, one might think, view knowledge in an adversarial manner, and scientists and engineers, who could be assumed to take a more positivist view.[60]

EMPLOYMENT

Taken together, age, gender, and field of education are not as important for the attitudes and values of risk professionals as is place of employment. For our respondents, where you work is strongly correlated to worldview. Cotgrove's research on the linkage between occupation and environmentalism has indicated that employment in the service sector rather than the production sector leads to strong proenvironmental views.[61] His definition of the service sector corresponds closely with the nonprofit sector. As we observed in Chapter 2, the majority of risk professionals are employed in this sector, especially the federal executive agencies. The private, for-profit sector is strongly represented by individuals who work for corporations, professional and trade associations, and the consulting and legal firms they employ. We would expect to find differences in support for elements of the competing paradigms between the public employees in government and not-for-profits and the private sector, encompassing companies and their associated infrastructure.

Place of employment is significantly related to each of our four items comprising the nature dimension of environmentalism. On each of these four, the strongest support for the new environmental outlook comes, not surprisingly, from those members of the risk profession working for environmental groups. For these people, the levels of rejection of the dominant social paradigm are strong and consistent. Slightly lower but still strong support for the new worldview comes from both executive and legislative branches of the federal government, with the non-EPA component of the executive branch having the highest average support for proenvironmental values. People employed by consulting and legal firms, think tanks, and universities show lower levels of support for the new paradigm, although majorities still favor each of the four items. Opposition to the environmentalist worldview comes from corporations and their related trade associations. Members of the risk profession based in these private sector organizations strongly disagree with the notion that humanity is abusing the environment and that we are seeing only the tip of the risk iceberg. They also are convinced that these risks often are exaggerated. It is of interest, however, that even those risk professionals employed by corporations agreed (55 percent of them, at least) that nature's balance is delicate and easily upset.

There are also significant linkages between employment and questions from each of the other three dimensions of environmentalism. More than a quarter of the people working in law and consulting firms, think tanks and universities, and corporations agreed with the statement that public involvement often leads to bad policy decisions. And these same people feel that business does a good job in protecting us from hazards, which, as noted above, runs against the overall perception of our respondents. A majority of the risk professionals working for the EPA (57.6 percent) also agreed with this statement. Finally, views of a zero-risk carcinogen standard are related strongly to employment. Most environmental group employees (55.5 percent) agree with the use of such a criterion, while the overall sentiment of the risk professionals is in opposition and fully nine-tenths of corporate employees reject it.

In the late 1960s and early 1970s, it was often suggested that environmental issues were bipartisan. Comparison of the risk professionals' political ideology with their values belies that argument. Overall, our respondents view themselves as liberals. Over 57 percent identify themselves as "very liberal" or "liberal," while only 13.3 percent report they are "very conservative" or "conservative." This self-reported ideology appears to have the strongest links to the environmental attitudes and values of risk professionals. The political value system of our respondents appears to be an important correlate of the new environmental paradigm. While political ideology is related to each of the four dimensions of environmentalism, the strongest connections are found on the nature and economy dimensions.

As could be expected, the strength of support for the new environmental paradigm comes from those respondents who characterized themselves as either very liberal or liberal. For example, on the question of whether we are seeing only the tip of the iceberg with regard to technological risk, 88.5 percent of those with a very liberal self-reported ideology agreed with the statement, as did 74 percent of liberals. Only 25 percent of very conservative and 36.4 percent of conservative respondents agreed. The same pattern holds across the range of environmental issues, and on five items (whether technology should be relatively uninhibited, whether business does a good job, whether humanity is abusing the environment, whether the risks of technology are exaggerated, and whether a zero-risk approach should be undertaken) the liberal—conservative cleavages are even more dramatic.

Given this configuration of ideology-attitude relationships, the correlates of political ideology are worth considering. Predictably, most of our self-identifying liberals tend to be under 44 years of age, work in environmental groups, consulting firms, or the federal government, and have educational backgrounds either at the bachelor's degree level or below, or graduate work in the social sciences and humanities. Perhaps even more interesting are the variations on this theme. Even among those risk professionals over 44 years of age, almost half (47 percent) still characterize themselves as liberal in outlook. Almost as striking is the fact that almost one-third of our respondents who work in corporations (31.3 percent) or in think tanks and universities (31.6 percent) also have liberal ideological frameworks. This raises the possibility that ideology might play a role in facilitating communication across or within various institutional settings.

Conclusion

Overall, the risk professionals show considerable support for the new environmental paradigm, and it may be that this shared worldview is a basis of unity within the policy system. But there are important exceptions to a consensus among our respondents. Like the difference in research resources that separates environmental organizations from other actors, these exceptions have important implications for the dynamics of the policy system.

The risk professionals strongly endorse the environmental worldview with regard to human relationships to nature and with regard to the problem of the market. Most participants in the risk policy system accept the fragility of nature and the threats posed by human activity. This implies that the problems addressed by the system are quite serious. There also seems to be agreement that the market cannot solve these problems. But there is much less consensus about the efficacy and fairness of the political process and of the role of science in this process. So while most members of the risk policy system share beliefs about the magnitude of the problem and how it *cannot* be remedied, there is much less continuity of belief in terms of how the problem *can* be resolved. We explore this theme in more detail in Chapter 4.

If there is a general agreement among risk professionals on the validity of the new environmental paradigm, there are some in the system who take exception to this worldview. Gouldner's work on the new class suggests that educational background is an important source of this kind of variation. But our results do not show any strong effect of education on worldview. Likewise, gender and age, which are determinants of environmental attitudes among the general population, have only slight discriminatory power among our respondents. Instead, place of employment seems to be the strongest determinant of a risk professional's worldview.

In Chapter 2, we observed that environmental organizations are different than other actors in the risk policy system because they have less in-house research capability. Here we find that it is the corporations and trade associations that are the "odd man out." While there is a consensus on most dimensions of environmentalism among most members of the risk policy system, risk professionals working for corporations and trade associations depart sharply from the majority of our respondents on most of these items. Indeed, while there is some variation across other employment categories, it is the rejection of the new environmental paradigm by representatives of the private sector that dominates the correlation between employment and ideology. The representatives of corporations and trade associations have developed a worldview dramatically at odds with the outlook of most other participants in the risk policy system. To help explain this disjuncture, it is important to consider briefly the relationship between ideology and the dynamics of a policy system.

In her recent book on risk, Mary Douglas suggests that variation in ideologies can be explained in terms of the "latent functions" they serve. She suggests that environmental organizations, like cults, adopt a worldview of "cosmic doom" in order to perform the latent function of maintaining their membership. In her words:

> This argument claims that the organizations which are most keenly alert to low-probability, high-consequence danger are religious sects and communes (notoriously millennialist and apt to prophesy doom) and also any political lobbies, new political movements, and public interest groups not able to provide special selective benefits for their members. The more difficulty they have in holding their membership together and getting common dues paid, the more they are tempted to invoke cosmic plot and to impeach a traitor. The doom-laden cosmos is part of the functioning of an organizational type whose latent goals present a particularly acute problem.[62]

According to this view, environmentalists behave like "Chicken Little," proclaiming doom to gain attention and maintain otherwise fragile coalitions. The argument could be generalized to include other members of the risk policy system whose budget and prestige depend on environmental issues being at the forefront of the national political agenda. Our empirical results are consistent with this position, since the risk professionals do consider environmental problems important and feel that government intervention, and thus risk policy, is critical to their solution. But an argument about the functions of ideology provides little insight into the dynamics of a policy system, and seems to become little more than the labeling of one side or another in the debate. For example, rather than invoking the notion of "cosmic doom" and organizational maintenance to explain the position of environmentalists, it is equally reasonable to argue that representatives of the private sector have adopted a Pollyanna stance, denying the sense of serious threat that is a consensus among other members of the policy system. If the system accepts the idea that environmental risks are minimal, regulation will be limited and industry can externalize some environmental costs of production. This fulfills a manifest function for the private sector—the need to maximize profit.

We find it more fruitful to focus on the interplay between ideology and the strategy and tactics of actors in the policy system.[63] In our view, the tactics and ideology of an actor in the policy system tend to be consistent, with each shaping the other in dynamic interplay within the system. Consider the positions taken by environmental groups and corporations as the risk policy system has evolved. During the 1960s, environmental problems were not a central component of the national policy agenda. As evidence about environmental disruption accumulated, environmentalists evoked images of "ecocide" and conducted dramatic public actions, such as mass demonstrations and teach-ins. These efforts served to develop public awareness of environmental problems and forced the development of the risk policy system. We suspect that a survey of the system during that period would find sharp differences in worldview between environmental organization representatives and *both* government officials and private sector employees. But as scientific knowledge has increased, most members of the growing policy system have come to acknowledge its critical nature. In turn, environmental organizations have moderated their rhetoric and have increasingly focused attention and effort on concrete policy issues. They have been able to move from "consciousness raising" to policy because they have been reasonably successful in altering the perceptions of the general public and most other participants in the policy system. Having won major battles over ideology, environmentalists now fight contests on specific policy concerns.

In contrast, the initial strategy used by the private sector to stop regulatory intrusion into their domain was to deny the existence of a problem. This was reasonable enough twenty years ago, but the strategy has lost credibility as evidence of environmental damage has been collected and digested. Thus, a newer, multifaceted strategy: deny that the problems generated by production processes are serious, argue that any risks that are generated have been exaggerated, and call for a cautious risk policy approach that emphasizes the accumulation of "good science" prior to taking action. The more polemical advocates of this argument go so far as to label environmentalists paranoid.[64] The less rhetorical version of the argument suggests that society simply has not been rational in choosing which environmental risks to regulate, that the risk policy system focuses most attention on some inconsequential items while ignoring other major hazards.[65] From a strategic perspective, it is no surprise that private sector actors hold a very different worldview than other members of the environmental health and safety policy system. If they adopted the environmentalist perspective in any substantial way, they would face a sharp inconsistency between the general arguments about risk they must make as part of their jobs and their belief system itself.

This analysis of strategy and ideology suggests that we turn our attention to the "establishment" perspective. The new class worldview has identified both commonalities and cleavages among the risk professionals. Whatever ideological consensus exists among our respondents, the establishment perspective suggests that they may be of little relevance to the workings of the policy system if all actors adopt common views on either specific policy issues or on how the policy process should be managed. Whatever the overall worldview of the risk policy system, it is the details of the policy process that actually affect both the production process of corporations and the quality of the environment.

Further questions about the character of the political process derive from a different perspective—that of the establishment. These issues are the subject of Chapter 4.

Chapter 4 Risk Professionals as an Establishment

In the late 1960s and early 1970s, environmentalists joined those protesting the war in Vietnam to accuse "the establishment" of promoting militarism and the exploitation of both people and the natural environment. The establishment, in the view of the activists of that period, was composed of politicians and government officials, including the military, officials in major corporations, and the leaders of other influential organizations. These individuals were seen as controlling the key institutions of American society and of using these institutions to promote their views. In particular, they were perceived as being able to define the terms of political debate, and of determining whether or not a point of view was accorded legitimacy.

While critiques of the establishment seem a bit less common than they were fifteen or twenty years ago, the idea that the terms of policy debates are set by a small number of actors who share a common worldview has been an ongoing theme in political commentary since World War II. President Eisenhower warned of dangers inherent in the "military-industrial complex," and any number of scholars have echoed this theme since then.[66] The establishment perspective on policy is similar to an elite view in that it suggests that effective power is held by a small fraction of the population. But establishment theory emphasizes the institutional character of that power. Members of an establishment work in a limited range of organizations and over time the interactions between those bodies become routine. In particular, a common set of problem definitions emerges, and debate is limited to issues that are consistent with those definitions. Certain kinds of policy positions and types of evidence or criteria regarding desirability of policy options are rejected a priori because they do not fit the problem definition used by the establishment. Members of the establishment may differ on the positions they ultimately take on policy issues, and on the worldview that drives these positions, but there is consensus about what issues and evidence are salient.

Considering risk professionals and the organizations in which they work as an establishment led us to ask questions about the environmental policy process. In this chapter we explore our respondents' views of that process. A number of writers have suggested that a risk establishment has emerged, but there is little consensus about its constituency. We begin, therefore, by considering some alternative views of the risk policy system as an establishment. We then turn to the risk professionals' views about problems with the environmental policy process, the sources of public controversy, and the mechanisms that might alleviate such controversies. The role of science in the environmental policy process is one of our central concerns, and we examine the risk professionals' perceptions of how science affects disputes among experts. We also consider their views of formal policy analysis methods, such as risk and cost-benefit analysis, and we examine how their viewpoints differ across different segments of the risk policy system.

Risk Establishments

The establishment, which attracted so much attention in the Vietnam era, was held to be composed primarily of government and industry leaders. It was argued that these people controlled vast resources which they used to manipulate the overall policy agenda as well as specific actions. This view contrasted the establishment with "challengers," typically voluntary organizations that grew out of social movements, especially environment and consumer groups.[67] From this perspective, the risk establishment is composed of those working for regulatory agencies and regulated industries. Government and industry officials may differ on policy specifics, but they agree on the terms of the debate and that consensus serves to keep environmental groups outside the policy process, or at least at the margin.

At the other end of the spectrum, some radical environmentalists have suggested that there is an environmental establishment, and that it incorporates industry, government, and environmental groups. As was mentioned in the previous chapter, this is the kind of critique offered by Foreman, who suggests that regular participation in the policy system causes environmental lobbyists to develop an establishment perspective consistent with that of industry and government.[68]

In recent years, some scholars have developed a variation on these themes by arguing that establishments have developed on *both sides* of most major environmental issues, including policies toward risk. Douglas and Wildavsky describe the idea of institutionalized conflict over environmental hazards as follows:

> Each side in the current debate is thought by the other to be serving the interests of preferred social institutions. Whether the reference is to the industrial establishment or the *"danger establishment"* that lobbies against it, each takes the arguments of the other to be self-serving and therefore false [emphasis added].[69]

This view of two contending establishments provides a useful insight when emphasizing the institutionalized character of environmentalist and industry participation in the policy process. But it seems misleading in two regards. First, the dichotomy implies equal, opposed establishments. This ignores the substantial difference in resources available to the two groups. Second, it fails to take into account the role of government itself. A central facet of environmental health and safety risk debates is that both corporate and environmental interests suspect an alliance between government and the other side. Thus, a lobbyist for the construction industry could, in the days of the Carter administration, argue of EPA that "the environmentalists were just in control down there. They put in all these harassing regulations and spent billions of dollars and they didn't accomplish a damn thing. You could see the awful waste. They just wanted to control everything."[70] On the other side of the coin, Joan Claybrook and the staff of Public Citizen, speaking of the same agency some three years later, gave the following account of events: "In 1981, the nation's environmental laws were in the hands of a president who accused the trees of causing air pollution, a budget director who bragged about his contempt for environmental laws, and a group of former employees and friends of polluting industries, whose previous jobs found them skirting or condemning the laws that they were now entrusted with executing."[71]

Rather than focusing on establishments structured around political positions, Steve Rayner suggests three types of "institutional cultures" that seem to be important in shaping policy positions: competitive/market, bureaucratic/hierarchical, and egalitarian. We consider the cultures as representing three establishments: industry, government, and environmental organizations, each with an internal consensus on how the policy process should be structured. Each of these establishments can be identified, in part, by their views on risk-taking, preferred spread of risks and costs, favored means of obtaining consent, and the like. In Rayner's words, "the social organization of the institutions and communities concerned, rather than the risks themselves, determine the policy process."[72]

Of course, Rayner's thesis could be expanded to move beyond a trichotomy. There may be many institutionalized cultures within the risk policy system. For example, the natural scientists in a large agency, such as EPA, may be buffered from the pressures that shape the positions of policy specialists, such as attorneys. It is this potential for complexity that leads us to examine differences in policy positions across segments of the risk system.

Before turning to our respondents' views, it is worth noting the difference between the analysis in this chapter and that of Chapter 3. There we focus on the worldview, or the fundamental and very general attitudes of the risk professionals toward the environment. Here the analysis shifts focus. An establishment perspective suggests that the kind of environmental cleavages we outlined in the previous chapter may be irrelevant to the policy process. If environmentalists and corporate employees differ in fundamental worldview but have reached a consensus on how policy debates should be resolved, then differences in paradigms may be of limited significance. This is because the rules of the debate may strongly influence, if not determine, the policy outcome. Such consensus will act to confine conflict over policy. But because such rules define the importance of key resources and are of immense consequence to policy outcome, we anticipate that there will be differences in views of the policy process just as there were differences in ideology. Thus, in this chapter we examine our respondents' policy positions and their attitudes on specific issues in the environmental policy process. In effect, we focus on the very language of policy debates and the way in which those positions differ across groups.

Environmental Policy Controversies

Two perspectives seem common in the analysis of scientific and technological controversies. The first, and dominant, is what Harold Linstone calls the "usual perspective" of decision making. It is characterized by defining policy problems in an abstract fashion, optimism that such problems can be solved, optimization, reductionism, reliance on data and models, quantification of information, assumptions of the objectivity of the scientist, ignoring the individual, and viewing time as linear movement.[73] The second encompasses a wide variety of critiques of the usual perspective, but there are several common threads across critical analyses. For one thing, the critiques tend to argue that organizational and personal views are underemphasized in the usual perspective. Without consideration of these views, it is argued, values such as justice, equity, or morality are given little weight. In other words, this argument suggests that certain "ethical bases" tend to be of little significance in the usual perspective.[74]

By itself, this normative element of the critique might well be ignored. But, critics posit, there is a direct connection between the elimination of ethical considerations and the manner in which policymakers approach the resolution of policy problems. This is especially the case for problems that have a high scientific or technical content, such as environmental health and safety. Critics maintain that in these areas the analytical tools advocated by the usual perspective, such as cost-benefit analysis or risk analysis, artificially set values on human life, disguise the distribution of costs and risks throughout the society, usually to the disadvantage of the general public, are easily abused by those seeking to manipulate the policy process, and in any event end up trying to compare phenomena that are not comparable.[75]

Defenders of the usual perspective typically respond to this attack by arguing that it is "irrational" or "emotional," and by asserting that our society must continue to try to develop better policy analysis techniques, whatever the current limitations. In the words of William Lowrance, "the first challenge is to develop analytic approaches that directly inform, illuminate, and aid decisionmaking that affects the public. Although we can't expect perfectly 'rational' public decisions, we must continue to try to develop rational perspective, including perspective on our irrationalities."[76]

In Chapter 1 we discussed the crucial role that scientific information and formal policy analysis play in environmental health and safety policy. The choice of analysis methods, the rules of the debate, are consequential for the choices made. And a strong belief in the validity of "rational" policy methods also suggests the irrationality of those who do not rely on such approaches, discounts the value of some factors, such as public opinion, which are not a part of formal analysis, so views on methods are associated with views on other aspects of the policy process. To the extent that risk professionals constitute a single establishment, we expect them to hold common views on the policy process. If there are multiple establishments, then our respondents will be divided in their views on methods and the process, even as the policy literature is divided on those issues.

Competing Views of Environmental Controversies

First we examine our respondents' perceptions of the biggest problems with the environmental policy process. We provided an open-ended question which allowed each respondent to describe a range of policy process problems. We limited our analysis to the three most important problems listed by each of the respondents. The questions elicited a wide variety of responses, but in general the risk professionals tend to view the absence of a conflict resolution mechanism, the lack of a federal environmental policy strategy, bad legal frameworks, no consensus about risk and the lack of data as the biggest problems. The most common response was that the process was too polarized and adversarial, with few conflict resolution mechanisms. Our respondents often said that this polarization prevents the public from understanding the issues. For instance, the associate director of a major corporation stated: "We are stalemated regarding constructive change between environmental and industrial communities. Any important issues aren't addressed or resolved." In a similar vein, a policy analyst at EPA cited the major problem as "the lack of communication between the various factions—industry, environmental organizations, regulators and politicians," noting that "they're like ships passing in the night—or colliding." They do not see as very serious the size of environmental problems, low levels of funding, or the role of special interests.

In terms of the various models of decision making, these results are a mixed bag. Certainly proponents of the usual perspective have been highly critical of the "drift" of U.S. science policy strategies in recent decades and the adverse consequences of bending technical analysis to narrowly legalistic purposes.[77] Reliance on data is a key to this outlook. But conflict resolution and consensus concerns are more typically associated with alternative perspectives or, to use Linstone's terminology again, the "organizational" or "personal" perspectives.[78] Moreover, the low rating of the funding issue seems to be a contradiction to the usual perspective. On the other hand, low ratings for the size of the problem and the role of special interests seem to be incompatible with many of the alternative views of the policy process.

This kind of complexity on open-ended responses was not unexpected. To provide some clarification, we asked respondents to assess the importance of five major sources of environmental controversy:

1. Misunderstandings and fears on the part of the public.
2. An uneven distribution of net risks and benefits in which those who benefit from a situation do not bear the costs.
3. Differences in individual values regarding risk-taking and uncertainty.
4. Public mistrust of government.
5. Public mistrust of industry.

Each of the five is regarded as a "major source" by risk professionals, but the proportion of respondents classifying a source as major range from 53.1 to 76.7 percent. Two sources, public mistrust of industry (76.7 percent) and public fears and misunderstandings (72.4 percent) are mentioned as major factors much more often than the other items. Public mistrust of government (53.1 percent) is the least cited of the five. When asked to rank-order the five sources, however, misunderstandings and fears on the part of the public are viewed as the most significant source of controversies by 40.3 percent of respondents. Clearly the risk professionals are in line with the conventional wisdom, typical of the technical outlook of the usual perspective, that public scientific illiteracy is a major problem. Explanations for public misunderstanding range from "the result of insufficient education" (a trade association policy analyst), to "the press plays a large part in feeding misunderstanding" (an EPA official), to "environmental groups exacerbate what misunderstandings there are" (a corporate division director). This position is consistent with Kenneth Prewitt's observation that American science leaders feel that public misunderstanding of science "will work its way through the political process and emerge in such detrimental policies as wide fluctuations in science funding, political rather than scientific criteria in setting research priorities, unrealistic demands for quick practical results, and misguided regulations for accounting procedures."[79]

When asked what we should do to reduce the intensity of these policy controversies, a similar pattern emerges. We provided six options:

1. Provide the public with more accurate scientific information on environmental risks.
2. Strictly control communication between industry and government.
3. Provide public funding for intervenor groups, such as environmentalists.
4. Arrange mediation or other conflict resolution procedures outside of standard legal and regulatory procedures.
5. Arrange for compensation to gain support of those adversely affected by a policy.
6. Encourage political discussion to focus on value questions rather than technical issues.

A majority of our respondents feel that three of the six would reduce environmental policy controversy: provide more accurate scientific information to the public (80.9 percent responding that it would either "greatly reduce" or "reduce somewhat" policy controversies), arrange mediation or other conflict resolution procedures (82.4 percent), and make arrangements for compensation for those adversely affected (57.4 percent). The other three options received less than majority support. When forced to rank the six alternatives, by far the highest priority was attached to the provision of scientific information (38 percent ranking it first). Typical of the responses here, however, was the caveat that communicating such information to the general public is very difficult. A professor at a state university argued: "I'm not sure we want to reach 200 million people. We should try to reach the segment of the public which is knowledgeable and can absorb the technical information." Others focused on the problems of language barriers. A corporate expert in regulatory policy observed: "The public needs to know, but you need to put it into language that the public can understand." And a high-level administrator at the Nuclear Regulatory Commission raised the credibility issue when he pointed out: "Scientific information is accurate and abundant. The manner and by whom it's provided is the essential thing. It must be trustworthy." This represents strong support for the usual perspective. It is also worth noting that the somewhat surprising level of support for mediation efforts appears to be reflective of a general trend in the environmental policy arena, and one sign of the frustrations with the problems associated with current conflict resolution capabilities.[80] As a consultant said: "This is the great white hope. A lot of times, if you just get people to talk, it helps a lot."

Given the high priority attached to resolving environmental conflicts through increased communication of scientific information, it comes as no surprise that the risk professionals view scientific research as influential in the policy process. Almost 60 percent of our respondents rate science "extremely" or "moderately" influential. Moreover, more than half (53.3 percent) agree with the proposition that "good science" does change people's minds and only 13.8 percent respond that it does not. Again, there are a variety of rationales offered for the influence of science, ranging from "it defines the boundaries of debate, but it doesn't give answers" (an environmental group attorney), to "extremely influential, but not because people believe it, but because it has the cloak of credibility" (a trade association program director), to "extremely influential, but not well controlled" (an NRC official). This is a striking finding, since much of the recent literature in the field has focused on the very real difficulties of trying to alter public perceptions of risk through the provision of more reliable, valid, and credible data.[81]

However, the risk professionals are not as optimistic about the level of understanding of environmental science within the policy system. When asked their evaluation of policymakers' understanding of environmental science, only 42.4 percent of our respondents characterized this level of comprehension as "good" or "basic." This perception raises a serious question about the potential value of expertise in the policy system. If policymakers have limited understanding of science, then the power of scientific and technical experts would appear to be strengthened. Thus, we turn to a set of questions designed to examine the risk professionals' positions regarding the internal dynamics of controversies involving conflicting expertise.

We presented our respondents a list of five factors commonly cited in the literature as linked to conflicts between experts:

1. Experts "arguing past" each other by focusing on different points.
2. Ambiguities resulting from different assumptions or judgments.
3. Experts rejecting the validity of data discrepant with their position.
4. Alternative interpretations of the same information.
5. Polarization resulting from differences in politics, paradigms, or position.

Majorities of the risk professionals identify each of these as either "almost always" or "frequently" involved in such disputes. Three of the factors seem central to conflicting expertise: ambiguities resulting in different assumptions or judgments (supported by 93.8 percent of risk professionals), polarization resulting from differences in politics, paradigms, or position (cited by 91.1 percent), and alternative interpretations of the same information (87.8 percent). The other two factors are seen as less frequently involved. In other words, the risk professionals appear to see conflicts between experts more in terms of information problems (data ambiguities, interpretations, and paradigms) than outright rejection of data or focusing on different points. But this is not to say that our respondents may not find politics an important source of expert controversy. Rather, they may feel politics and values produce differences in paradigms, but in a subtle way that may not be seen by the experts. As a consultant in cancer research noted, "most scientists aren't aware of this and rarely admit to their value orientations, backgrounds, and emotional baggage." Overall, these results appear to be consistent with our earlier findings with respect to the risk professionals' positions on the sources of controversy and solutions to them.

If informational rather than personal or institutional factors are seen by our respondents as accounting for most expert conflicts, one would expect proposals to resolve such disputes to focus on data evaluation and processing mechanisms rather than more structural or ethical frameworks. Indeed, this is precisely the pattern of response we received when we asked respondents to rate the utility of three commonly suggested reforms:

1. Provide a code of professional practice and ethics within which experts could resolve disputes.
2. Have technical debates resolved through a peer review process.
3. Have disagreeing experts confront each other as adversaries before a panel of judges.

Risk professionals have much more faith in the traditional practice of allowing experts to rule on the merits of disputes through the process of peer review. Almost 79 percent said that a peer review process would be either "very" or "somewhat" useful for such a purpose. By contrast, the installation of a code of ethics or professional practice (36.9 percent) or implementation of an adjudicatory body (35.7 percent) receives markedly less support. As one would predict, the risk professionals tend to trust experts to resolve conflicts within scientific frameworks more than they favor a move toward internal professional controls or external adversarial procedures. This is no surprise, since peer review preserves the traditional autonomy of scientists while codes of conduct or "science courts" have been identified for some time as mechanisms for extending outside accountability over the expert community.[82]

Finally, we asked a series of questions about the role of technical analysis itself in the policy process. First, we wanted to know the position of risk professionals on the influence of formal techniques of analysis, such as risk and cost-benefit analysis. As was the case with several of our attitude and value items in the previous chapter, we can make comparisons with the work of Lynn.[83] A majority of our respondents (56.3 percent) see formal analysis as "very" or "moderately" influential, but this is not the overwhelming statement of faith we might have expected. However, when the question is narrowed to the topic of risk assessment itself, more support emerges. When we asked risk professionals whether they favored or opposed the use of formal risk analysis in environmental policy, they were strongly in favor of the use of the technique. Over 70 percent supported the use of risk assessment tools, while only 13.2 percent expressed opposition.

Support for formal risk analysis, however, does not translate into support for the centralization of these activities into a single federal organization. Our respondents are strongly opposed to the centralization idea, with 64.6 percent expressing opposition to the concept, while only 18.4 percent are in favor of it. Apparently the current decentralized, differentiated manner in which risk analyses are carried out does not strike the risk professionals as dysfunctional.

Cost-benefit analysis receives almost as much support as formal risk analysis. Some 63.3 percent of our respondents favored the use of cost-benefit tools in environmental policymaking. Asked why they favored or opposed its use, risk professionals offer a range of rationales. The most common reply is that cost-benefit techniques serve as an aid to decision, while the second most frequent answer is that such approaches enable the consideration of important economic factors. A high-level administrator in the Consumer Product Safety Commission effectively summarized this argument: "I favor it with a recognition of the limitations of what you're dealing with. It forces both the staff and the agencies to focus their attention and define which are the most important components of the decision. I don't favor it as a mathematical balancing tool. That is an abuse." And a director of a professional association came to a similar conclusion: "It produces a logical result within the boundaries of the question asked, leaves trails by which you can validate or rebut the outcomes, and permits you to make some trade off decisions." On the other hand, the third most common response, from those opposed to the technique, is that we are not able to quantify the phenomena typically incorporated into the cost-benefit framework. A senior attorney for an environmental organization gave the standard critique here: "Some values (e.g., effects on soils, buildings, etcetera) you can calculate. Others you can't—it's morally offensive (e.g., people's health, their lives, the value of forests, and a pristine vista). These you can't put a dollar value on." It is interesting to note that very few (5.5 percent) of the risk professionals give as their rationale the misuse of cost-benefit techniques, nor do many question the validity of the approach itself (3.0 percent).

The overall support for cost-benefit analysis is similar to Lynn's findings. In her sample of occupational health and safety experts, those based in industry were highly supportive of the tool (71 percent were in favor), and more than half (53 percent) of the university experts expressed support. But only 37 percent of her government respondents agreed with this assessment.[84]

The Language of Environmental Policy

Related to the use of formal analytical techniques is a set of issues that we call the language of environmental policy. Here the focus is on debates surrounding various sources of evidence (from traditional or folk wisdom through experiments on humans or nonhuman organisms to epidemiological surveys), modes of assembling evidence (various conditions of exposure, problems of identifying adverse effects, relating exposure to effect, and estimating overall risk), problems of inference (relating cause to effect, extrapolating from animals to humans, etcetera), and expressing risk (probability and magnitude measures) in a meaningful form.[85] These together define what sorts of scientific information should be used in the policy process and thus determine what elements of "language" are seen as legitimate components of policy debates.

COMPETING VIEWS OF THE LANGUAGE OF ENVIRONMENTAL POLICY

Our first question in this area asked risk professionals their view of the use of short-term, high-dose animal studies as a basis for environmental regulation. We found broad acceptance of such studies. Almost 70 percent of our respondents favor the use of animal studies. Probed as to why, their responses are most often (33.5 percent) statements to the effect that these studies are all we have. A smaller group (21.4 percent) rationalizes the use of animal studies as a screening device, or "first cut" in risk analysis. On the negative side, the most common response emphasizes the extrapolation problems of such studies (13.7 percent). It is noteworthy that very few (2.7 percent) respond in terms of the abuse potential of animal studies. On balance, our respondents appear to agree with the U.S. Office of Technology Assessment's assertion that despite major obstacles most expert opinion supports the conclusion that the testing of laboratory animals "provides reliable information about carcinogenicity."[86]

A second major evidence-related question had to do with respondents' opinions regarding threshold levels for carcinogens. Here their views are quite divided. Some 47.8 percent answer in the negative to our query, while only 35.7 percent are supportive of the threshold concept. A critical 16.5 percent fall into the "probably/maybe" category. Clearly the entire question of thresholds has yet to be resolved among risk professionals. This is not at all surprising when one considers Walter Rosenbaum's assessment that there appear to be "Republican and Democratic theories of genetic chemistry," since the last two administrations have used conflicting interpretations of carcinogenic thresholds for regulating substances such as pesticides.[87]

Our third question focused on the public's sensitivity to risk evidence. Some authors have suggested that American society has become overly sensitive to risk, and that we now expect to be sheltered from almost all hazards.[88] Others argue that society simply is becoming more aware of risks and that we are now starting to take realistic precautions.[89] Our respondents do not agree with the idea of an overly sensitive, risk-averse population. Only 16.2 percent support this line of thought. Fully 50.5 percent support the view of a society more aware of the risks it faces. One-third of the risk professionals perceive a combination of both factors at work in environmental health and safety controversies—sensitivity increases at the same time that awareness heightens.

We should note that Lynn also explored the issues of animal studies and thresholds, but she used slightly different questions. Her industry respondents were predictably highly negative about the utility of animal studies, but they were highly supportive of the threshold concept. The reverse pattern characterized both government and university experts.[90]

Aside from policy concerns surrounding sources and uses of evidence, perhaps the next most controversial part of the language of environmental policy has to do with the valuation of life. On the general question of whether society must make an effort to place an economic value on human life in order to allocate scarce resources, the majority (59.9 percent) disagrees. An attorney for a law firm expressed disagreement because "economists think this way in order to make their models work. They are more interested in the symmetry of their models than in the societal issues involved." And an environmental organization attorney was even more critical, noting that "no economic activity should be based on human sacrifice. I reject the notion that corporate profits should be made at the expense of human lives." Thus, it appears that risk professionals are not convinced by the standard argument made by advocates of economic determinations of the value of life—that no matter how such a process may offend "moral sensitivities," a greater danger is that "these trade-offs will be made without systematic analysis."[91]

We also asked how the risk professionals evaluated particular methods to place an economic value on life. When offered a choice of three major techniques—"earnings lost," "individual willingness to pay," and "wage differentials"—a larger percentage of our respondents opt for asking the individuals how much they would be willing to pay to reduce the probability of death or disability (29.8 percent) than would compute the amount of earnings that would be lost in the case of premature death or disability and equate this with the value of life (20.2 percent). But, consistent with the overall disagreement with the setting of an economic value, 37.5 percent of risk professionals answer "none" of the techniques would be selected.

On this set of questions, Lynn's findings are strikingly similar to our own. Her occupational health and safety experts manifest the same pattern of hostility toward placing a value on human life, and show even more resistance to the dominant methods used for such valuations (almost half were dissatisfied with all three approaches).[92]

A related question in our survey asked about three very different ways to determine the distribution of risks in technical analysis: allowing people to make their own choices; calculating aggregate societal costs and benefits; or focusing on whether a particular group bears a disproportionate share of the risks. Again, the risk professionals evidence cynicism about cost-benefit calculations or reliance on market forces as determinants of risk policy. A majority of our respondents (50.2 percent) support the third option, which calls for identification of any disproportionate burden. Each of the other two options is supported by 18.4 percent of the risk professionals.

Finally we asked a question about funding. We wanted to know whether our respondents would increase, decrease, or maintain the same level of federal spending on improving and protecting the environment. Not surprisingly, almost 81 percent of the risk professionals expressed a desire to have the level of environmental protection spending increased, and only 1.5 percent said they would prefer to have it reduced. Whatever the concerns about how environmental science and policy decisions are made, it is certain that this group of people view increased federal support as a positive influence.

As we anticipated, the risk professionals exhibit a mixed-response pattern to our questions about environmental policy. On the one hand, respondents voice the usual perspective's positivist view of the value of scientific information in the policy process, and they are generally supportive of the traditional mechanisms of assessing scientific data, such as peer review. Likewise, they think technical analysis is of influence in the policy process and they are optimistic about the ability of this kind of information to alter people's perceptions of environmental issues. They believe in the utility of risk assessment and cost-benefit analysis as a policy analytical technique and in suggested conflict resolution mechanisms, such as mediation. But there is another side to the coin. This group of individuals is relatively negative when assessing policymakers' comprehension of technical information, and while they want work in the field to continue and are willing to spend more money on environmental protection in the future, they do not support centralization schemes. Moreover, the risk professionals are highly critical of much of the theoretical base of cost-benefit analysis and of the utility of economic approaches to the valuation of life in particular. Thus, the usual perspective's acceptance is subject to major exceptions.

Possible Explanations for Environmental Policy Positions

Given the complexity of responses on policy positions, we now turn to the examination of the factors that influence them. As we observed at the start of this chapter, the literature suggests that these differences should be strongly linked to institutional factors. Thus, we would expect our independent variables of place of employment and field of education to be more influential in explaining the policy positions of risk professionals than the other three factors—age, gender, and ideology.

AGE

In fact, age is less correlated with environmental policy questions than with environmentalism. The significant linkages are concentrated in one area, in this case the use of formal analysis. In particular, younger risk professionals are more negatively disposed toward the use of both risk and cost-benefit analysis. Other important relationships between age and policy position include positions on peer review, which our younger respondents find more useful than the older risk professionals, views of the most appropriate method to determine the distribution of risk, which are all rejected by a larger percentage of our younger *and* older professionals, higher levels of support among younger individuals for the position that society has become more aware of risks, rather than having become more sensitive, and a lower percentage of younger risk professionals categorizing misunderstanding and fears as a major source of environmental controversies.

These are not surprising findings when one examines the profile of our "under 35" group of risk professionals and compares it to the older (35–44, over 44) groups. The younger professionals tend to have relatively less education, as would be expected (almost 29 percent of them have a bachelor's degree or less) and of those who have done graduate work about half have law degrees. This low proportion of scientific and technical educational backgrounds may help explain the relatively low level of support for rational analytical techniques—a point that is examined later in the discussion of education field and policy position. Note also that there are moderate correlations between age and three of the other independent variables (gender, employment, and field of education).

GENDER

There is almost no connection between gender and our policy questions. Only on the issue of favoring risk assessment did gender play an important role. The women we interviewed are less supportive of the use of risk assessment than are the male members of the risk profession. Although a clear majority of the entire sample supports the use of the technique, women are much more inclined to hedge their bets than men; over one-quarter of them say "it depends," or give a mixed response. Less than half as many men give such a response. Gender did show up as important on three additional questions: women are much more inclined to say that public mistrust of government is a major source of controversy; that experts arguing past each other is *not* important for disputes; and that spending for protecting the environment should be increased. As was the case with age, gender is significantly related to three of the other independent variables—age (as already mentioned), education field, and self-reported ideology.

FIELD OF EDUCATION

As was the case with environmentalism, we thought we would find policy differences between risk professionals according to their educational training. In particular, we anticipated differences between those individuals trained in fields central to the risk *assessment* function (the hard sciences and engineering) and those with educational backgrounds more essential to risk *management* activities (law and the social sciences). In fact, educational field is more important for determining views on policy questions than it was in determining environmentalist values and attitudes.

The strongest relationships exist for policy positions having to do with sources of environmental controversy and ways to resolve disputes between experts. Those individuals who have graduate degrees in the sciences or engineering, business or economics, medicine or public health, and biology or ecology are more likely to take the position that public misunderstanding is a major source of controversy than are those with bachelor's degrees or less, law school graduates, and persons with graduate degrees in the humanities or social sciences. The same pattern persists when respondents were asked to identify the most important source of controversies. On the question of dispute resolution, two items are significantly linked to field of education: peer review and codes of practice. Predictably, people with graduate degrees in science and engineering are strong supporters of peer review, but it is somewhat of a surprise to find that those with a bachelor's degree or less are even stronger supporters. On the use of codes of practice, a more predictable pattern emerges. Again, respondents with a bachelor's degree or less are supportive, but they are joined by graduates in the humanities and social sciences as the major advocates of this policy option. These same three groups also are the strongest backers of the view that experts arguing past each other are a key source of expert disputes.

Four additional items elicited significant linkages to our education field variable, and there is some consistency across them. As we have seen, the risk professionals are divided on the issues of the utility of cost-benefit analysis and the valuation of life. As would be expected, individuals trained in business or economics are the most positive on both questions, while opposition comes from medical and public health professionals on the cost-benefit issue and from those with bachelor's degrees or less, lawyers, and humanities and social sciences graduates on the issue of valuation of life. The use of animal studies generates a different cleavage. Here medical and public health graduates are joined by business and economics graduates as the strongest backers of the use of such studies, while opposition comes from people with bachelor's degrees or less and individuals trained in biology or ecology. Finally, on the issue of experts arguing past each other as a source of disputes, biologists and ecologists, along with those with a bachelor's degree or less tend to agree with this assessment, while scientists and engineers, along with those trained in the humanities or social sciences, tend to disagree the most often.

EMPLOYMENT

Employment is a better predictor of policy position than of environmentalism. Here the most consistent pattern of responses is that for the role of technical analysis in the policy process. Place of employment is significantly linked to differences in the policy positions of our respondents on the use of both risk and cost-benefit analysis, and to several of the issues surrounding the language of environmental politics. Employees of federal agencies including EPA, corporations, and think tanks and universities are the most optimistic about the utility of risk analytical tools (with over 75 percent of each group supporting the use of such techniques), while environmentalists and congressional workers show the lowest levels of support. The same holds for optimism about cost-benefit analysis, although representatives of legal and consulting firms join environmentalists and legislative branch employees at the low end of the support spectrum on this item. And this pattern continues across most of the other items for which employment is a major factor.

The issue of sources of environmental controversy elicits similar results. The same coalition that supports the two technical analytical approaches also takes the position that public misunderstanding and fear are a major source of controversy and in fact are the most important source (joined in the latter opinion by legal and consulting firm employees). Predictably, the provision of more accurate information as a response to controversies is advanced by roughly the same coalition, although here congressional as well as legal and consulting firm employees are also in agreement. Likewise, EPA, think tank and university, and corporate workers are in agreement about the low potential for intervenor funding to reduce controversies, while representatives of environmental groups are the most optimistic about this policy alternative. There is little of the pattern evidenced on the issue of mediation as a conflict resolution mechanism, however. Although environmentalists are the most skeptical, almost 70 percent of them express optimism.

Two things are striking about the responses to the use of technical analysis and related sources of evidence, lines of investigation, and modes of assembling information. First, the pattern of responses for EPA and corporate employees are very similar. Any number of explanations might account for this phenomenon, but the most obvious would be the "modified capture" of EPA by corporate interests during the tenure of the Reagan administration. In recent years, the agency seems to have shifted from reflecting the interests of environmental groups to adopting a strategy designed to coopt its opposition rather than supporting its supporters.[93] Second, and possibly related to this notion of EPA-corporate convergence, the policy positions of environmental organizations are more similar to those of congressional employees than any other group. But these patterns are not repeated when other items are considered. On questions about how well policymakers understand science, whether an adversary conflict resolution procedure should be adopted, why animal studies should be used, whether there are carcinogenic thresholds, if society is more aware of risks, and the utility of valuation of human life, there are no clear alliances among institutions. EPA and corporate workers generally part company on these issues, especially on the level of science understanding by policymakers (with EPA personnel more than twice as positive as corporate employees), whether cancer-causing thresholds exist (with corporate workers almost three times as likely to answer yes), and whether we must place a value on human life (with almost 70 percent of EPA personnel responding in the negative, compared to only 38 percent of corporate risk professionals). Similarly, environmentalists have more in common with EPA employees on questions about why animal studies should be used and on the appeal of adversary dispute resolution approaches.

IDEOLOGY

Self-reported ideology appears to have as much or more to do with the policy positions of risk professionals as with their attitudes toward environmentalism. There are important relationships between self-reported ideology and seventeen of our policy items. Key linkages exist between the respondents' ideology and positions on the sources of scientific and technical controversy, with liberals tending to view public understanding as less important and value differences as more important than do conservatives. Similarly, liberals are more prone than conservatives to believe that controlling government–industry communications and providing intervenor funding are options likely to reduce such controversies.

As was the case with age, gender, and place of employment, ideology is linked to risk professionals' positions on the utility of risk analysis. Fully 100 percent of those identifying themselves as "very conservative" and 91 percent of "conservatives" favor the approach, while only 52 percent of "very liberal" and 56.8 percent of "liberal" respondents concur. Other items strongly connected to ideology include the utility of peer review as a dispute resolution mechanism (conservatives are much more positively disposed toward this proposal than are liberals), belief in thresholds for carcinogens (again, with conservatives more likely to accept the idea), the degree to which our society has become overly sensitive to risks (liberals disagreeing, and asserting that society is more aware, while conservatives take the opposite position), whether it is necessary to place a value on human life (liberals disagreeing, while conservatives support the notion), and the proper method for determining the distribution of risks (conservatives preferring the use of earnings lost or willingness to pay, while liberals advocate wage differentials).

Conclusion

In the last chapter, we found that there is a common worldview among a majority of the risk professionals. The establishment perspective suggested that there would be general agreement on the ways in which risk policy should be formulated, on the reasons for problems in the process, and on the kinds of techniques and evidence that should be used in developing and implementing policy. What we have found is a rather complex mix of agreement and disagreement on these issues.

Professional socialization, as reflected in educational background, has much more effect on views of the policy process than on basic worldview. Individuals trained in the natural sciences and especially those trained in economics and business are much more likely to attribute controversy to public misunderstanding than other participants in the risk policy system. They also favor peer review. Both of these positions legitimate the role of technical expertise in the policy process and thus enhance the potential power of those who possess that expertise. We do not view these positions as narrowly self-serving but as an indication of the consistency between attitudes and interests resulting from their interplay in the policy system.

Much as we expected, there are sharp differences in policy attitudes across organizations in the system, but these differences are rather complex. An establishment of executive branch officials, private sector representatives, and individuals working at think tanks and universities has emerged around the use of technical analysis and a belief that public ignorance generates controversy. Participation in this establishment is explicable in terms of the differing needs of each institutional actor within the policy system. In recent years federal regulators have been heavily influenced by the Reagan administration, which has tried to restrict environmental regulation through the increased use of formal policy analysis methods. In addition to this recent top-down pressure, formalization of policy decision making always has great appeal to government officials when there is reason to believe the decisions will be controversial. Whatever the outcome of the decision-making process, officials can argue to opponents that formal analysis indicates a "rational" way to proceed, and thus legitimates the chosen course of action. Corporate interests also find formal analyses of value because they use them to press their argument that the risk policy system is overreacting to many environmental problems. The substantial scientific resources at the command of both government and the private sector make them reasonably confident that they can hold their own in debates that rest heavily on the use of rationalistic policy analysis methods. And the biases in formal policy analysis methods seem especially to favor corporate interests and the status quo in regulation.[94] The support for formal techniques on the part of those working in universities and think tanks probably results from their more traditional advocacy of policy analysis, and the desire to "tinker with the system" and advocate various governmental reforms, although it is also possible that the growth of corporate-university linkages may be developing more subtle alliances, which result in the convergence of roles and positions of technical experts across these institutional lines.[95]

In contrast, those who deal most with the public, have the strongest public support, and possess the least technical resources do not blame public ignorance for controversy and are relatively skeptical of formal methods of analysis. Discounting the public would cost environmentalists and Congress their principal resource in the policy system. In any event, both environmental groups and congressional participants are vulnerable to any policy debate that hinges on technical details, since they can be easily overwhelmed by the technical "firepower" brought to bear by experts.

On other policy issues no clear establishment has emerged. Federal regulatory officials and corporate representatives differ on issues related to animal studies, cancer thresholds, and valuation of human life. In short, it seems that there are elements of a federal-private sector establishment within the risk system, but it is a limited one. Issues about what we term the language of risk are much more cross-cutting, with weak alliances across types of actors differing from issue to issue.

Again, we find that cleavages within the risk policy system are based on organizational affiliation. In the next chapter we continue this emphasis on organizations by considering the policy community perspective. There we focus on the ways in which individuals form linkages across organizations, and how those linkages structure the policy system.

Chapter 5 Risk Professionals as a Policy Community

Our fourth perspective for examining the risk professionals emphasizes the importance of "policy communities." A recent analysis of the energy policy system defines a community in the following terms:

> Policy communities can be viewed as information networks that deal primarily with substantive information and operate with little regard for organizational or hierarchical position. Stable policy communities consist of actors and interests who are continuously engaged in obtaining, digesting, exchanging, or testing information. Thus a very important part of the process by which these policy communities function is communication—through word of mouth, discussions in the workplace, meetings sponsored by professional societies, and numerous informal ways.[96]

This perspective suggests that the environmental risk policy system may be thought of as a communication system and that the structure of communication linkages is critical to the performance of the system. The idea of communication as a central factor in environmental health and safety risk policy positions is attractive for several reasons. First, communication appears to be the essence of Washington politics. Some observers have even gone so far as to term communication links "Washington survival networks."[97] By "network" we mean the "lines of communication, the alternative express highways that people use to get things done."[98] Networking is, in the words of Stuart Langton, an "organizational strategy to serve the interests of different groups and their members more efficiently."[99] Whether the communication highways transmit opinions, studies, or orders, they define any network as an interacting entity and make the participating bodies behave as a system, rather than as a random aggregation of individuals and groups.

A second attractive characteristic of networks is that they perform a variety of purposes. They may help mobilize political power in an aggressive, advocacy fashion, and they may also be important mechanisms for the generation of new knowledge for members of participating organizations. But the primary focus of most networks is to create and maintain an "exchange" capability, in which a scarce resource, information, is "bartered" among participants.[100]

The third reason for focusing on networks is that they may have special significance for environmental politics. This is because, as many observers of this arena have noted, environmental groups work hard to facilitate the creation and maintenance of extensive networks. In Langton's words:

> Network process and structures are particularly relevant to environmental groups for three reasons. One is that few environmental groups have sufficient resources to achieve their goals without a lot of help from others. Another reason is that many issues of concern to environmental groups are of a crisis nature. Therefore, environmentalists must mobilize information, resources, and support very quickly—and networking practices are the best way to do this. A final reason is that environmental problem solving requires a great deal of institutional interdependence. In addition to working together for the reasons cited above, environmental groups must relate to many governmental agencies, businesses, educational institutions, and the media. Informal networking contacts with like-minded people in these institutions is frequently the best way of avoiding the inherent bureaucratic hassles and barriers we encounter when we want to get something from these institutions.[101]

What is perhaps underemphasized in these arguments is the common concern community members have with one area of policy problems. As John Kingdon has observed, community communication patterns within a policy system vary across actors, but all members share one thing: "their specialization and acquaintance with the issues in that particular policy area."[102] In fact, some scholars have come to view the attentiveness to common policy concerns as a more important factor in the creation and maintenance of policy "domains" than communication per se. The work of David Knoke and Edward Laumann, for example, indicates that in the energy and health policy domains, "the central relationship is the actors' similarities in their attentiveness to the set of policy issues."[103] Membership in such an "issue public" thus is specified by a "criterion of mutual relevance or common orientation among a set of consequential actors concerned with formulating, advocating, and selecting courses of action (i.e., policy options) that are intended to resolve the limited substantive problems in question."[104] Also key to this interpretation is the definition of actors in *institutional* terms—formal organizations that control essential resources are seen as the significant social actors.[105] This leads analysts to focus exclusively on organizations in examining policy systems. Their analysis assumes that organizations are stable entities with constant or slowly evolving policy positions, while individuals come and go and must conform to the view of the organization in all official matters.

We concur that attentiveness is a necessary part of participation in a policy system, but it is not sufficient. If the members of a policy system constitute a community, then they must have links to one another. These are the mechanisms through which policy is influenced. In this chapter we consider four types of linkages. The most obvious is direct verbal communication. Flows of personnel from one organization to another are a second important form of communication within a policy system. In addition to these tangible links, there are perceptual connections. Members of the policy system accord legitimacy to one another and hold views about the relative influence various members exert on policy. The perceptual links are part of the "glue" that holds a policy system together.

In examining these linkages, we focus on organizations rather than individuals. We do feel, however, that the assumption that organizations are the only salient units of analysis for studies of policy systems sometimes oversimplifies the complex interplay between individuals and organizations. But a community perspective, with its emphasis on communication in the risk policy system, calls for consideration of structures in addition to the individual. So, in this chapter, we emphasize the characteristics of organizations as well as those of the risk professionals.

Personal Contact

The most obvious and perhaps most important link between actors in the policy system is personal contact. Phone calls and meetings seem a central activity for members of exchange networks, whatever their formal responsibilities. Members of the network exchange views on proposed or existing policy. They discuss and critique research results. Allies confer on strategy, and adversaries probe for any informational advantage. By such communication, the community comes to speak in a shared language and to focus on similar issues, even though they may differ dramatically in their positions on these issues. For a new item to be added to the policy agenda, it usually must be filtered through this network. While indirect modes of communication, such as press releases, articles, and speeches, have the advantage of being "planned" channels, the "unplanned" face-to-face contacts, conferences, or phone calls to friends and colleagues appear to generate most of the information that is actually *used* in most organizations.[106]

We asked our respondents to indicate whether or not, in a typical month, they had talked to anyone at each of seventeen organizations or types of organizations. The risk professionals cited some thirty-nine different bodies with which they had such contact, and they specified an additional forty-two subunits of EPA. We have collapsed these categories to eight in order to improve comparability with the previous chapters, preserve confidentiality, and simplify presentation of results. Although this condensation reduces our ability to discuss in detail the full complexity of communication patterns, analysis of both the condensed and the detailed patterns yields the same general results.

Table 5 presents the pattern of communication among organizations in the risk policy system. It delineates the percentage of respondents working at each of the eight organizational groupings who talk to each type of organization. For example, all of our EPA respondents reported talking to other offices at EPA; 71

Table 5 Communication Flows Among Organizations in the Risk Policy System

Percent of Respondents Saying They Talk to the Organization in a Typical Month	Employer of Respondent								
	EPA	Corporations and Trade Associations	Other Executive Agencies	Congressional Staff and Support Organizations	Environmental Organizations	Labor, State and Local Government, Other	Law and Consulting Firms	Universities, Think Tanks, NRC/NAS	Prominence
EPA	<u>100.0</u>	85.0	75.9	64.0	74.1	66.7	78.8	81.0	75.1
Corporations	71.4	<u>97.5</u>	72.4	84.0	85.2	83.3	87.9	81.0	80.7
Other Federal Agencies	85.7	70.0	<u>96.6</u>	92.0	81.5	77.8	93.9	95.2	85.2
Congress	60.0	60.0	51.7	<u>92.0</u>	100.0	77.8	54.6	47.6	64.5
Environmental Organizations	71.4	55.0	44.8	76.0	<u>100.0</u>	66.7	66.7	61.9	63.2
Labor, State and Local Government	31.4	37.5	62.1	64.0	66.7	<u>66.7</u>	48.4	52.4	51.8
Law and Consulting Firms	68.6	80.0	72.4	52.0	77.8	50.0	<u>78.8</u>	42.9	63.4
Universities, Think Tanks, NAS/NRC	8.6	2.5	3.4	8.0	3.7	5.6	9.1	<u>14.3</u>	5.8
Outreach	56.7	55.7	54.7	62.8	69.9	61.1	62.8	66.0	
Number of Respondents	35	40	29	25	27	18	33	21	

percent of EPA respondents said they talked to corporations or trade associations; and 85 percent of corporate or trade association respondents reported talking to EPA.

The first point to be made about the summarized pattern of communication is that there is a very great deal of contact. The average "density" of communication, the average of all percentages in Table 5, is 64 percent. This can be interpreted by noting that if everyone in our sample reported they talked to every organizational group, the average density would be 100. Thus, nearly two-thirds of all possible communication links between organizations are present. The risk professionals appear to be a rather comprehensive community in this respect.

The bottom row of Table 5 displays the degree to which respondents working for an organizational group report making contact with organizations outside that group. It is the average of all percentages within the column, except the percentage along the diagonal, since that represents communication within the organizational group. It is therefore a measure of *outreach*. This percentage may be interpreted in the same manner as the percentages within the table. If every respondent at EPA reported conversation with every other organization, then the outreach percent would be 100; if they claimed no contact, the percentage would be zero.

Environmental groups have an outreach percentage of 70, the highest of any group. This is consistent with our earlier discussion of the importance of networks for these organizations. As we have emphasized, environmental groups employ relatively few scientists, and have had only limited ability to collect and analyze primary scientific data from epidemiological studies or laboratory experiments. To be sure, a few organizations, such as the Environmental Defense Fund and the Natural Resources Defense Council, have made substantial progress in increasing the size and quality of their technical staffs in order to expand the scope of in-house analyses, but this is still the exception to the rule.[107] As a consequence, environmental groups must turn to other sources of expertise. Indeed, this scarcity of resources applies to policy monitoring as well as scientific analysis. Many federal agencies, law and consulting firms, and corporation and trade associations subscribe to private services that monitor the press, the scientific literature, and regulatory and legislative activity. The cost of many such services may be beyond the reach of most environmental groups, so they may have to rely on personal contacts to a greater extent. Finally, the political strength of environmental organizations comes from translating the broad public support for environmental protection into specific policy initiatives. Such mobilization of clientele support requires extensive communication.

Think tanks and universities have the next most extensive outreach, making two-thirds of all links. These organizations produce more basic research (that is, knowledge for its own sake, rather than for some application) and more policy analyses, which, at least in theory, attempt to incorporate multiple perspectives on any particular debate. Both of these roles are facilitated by communication linkages. In fact, think tanks and universities perform such "open" functions that it may be something of a surprise to find them less involved in outreach than environmental groups. In the Washington environment, however, the academics who populate think tanks and universities suffer from some special obstacles to becoming members of any policy network. As Kingdon understates it: "In some Washington quarters, there is a distrust of, and even a disdain for, academic work." Because academic work may be seen as too theoretical or abstract, and because even empirically sound analyses or recommendations may prove politically untenable, academic outreach may be truncated.

Congress, law and consulting firms, and labor, state and local governments each have outreach scores a bit over 60 percent. We believe these similar levels of outreach can be attributed to different factors. Although congressional capability for in-house research has been expanding in recent years (by the creation of the Office of Technology Assessment and the expansion of the Library of Congress, General Accounting Office, and member and committee staff resources), and the environmental critique of modern technology has been an essential factor in the development of this infrastructure, it remains limited in scope.[108] The legislative branch, therefore, must contact other institutions to monitor scientific developments and to receive technical assistance in evaluating studies. On balance, Congress appears to be in an ideal central position to establish links to each of the other major components of the environmental health and safety community. There are few institutions with Congress's capability to bridge the gap between members of the basic science community and those institutions that set the goals of society. Yet in many ways these links have proven difficult to establish or maintain. According to George Brown, Jr., the Democratic representative from California who is the senior member of the House Science and Technology Committee:

> One of the pleasures, as well as frustrations, of serving in Congress is seeing the linkages between the different sectors of society. In a healthy, dynamic society, those linkages are strong, thereby ensuring constant communication and interaction. When those linkages become strained or severed, the health of society suffers. This is precisely the problem that has arisen with U.S. science and technology. Important linkages between basic scientific research and other activities of our society have been allowed to atrophy.[109]

Labor and state and local governments are engaged in outreach for reasons similar to environmental groups and Congress. They have limited scientific or technical resources, so are net consumers of information. In addition, they are groups that have political impact largely through their ability to mobilize broad support and to form coalitions. Law and consulting firms, in contrast, are producers of information. But they are dependent upon a continued flow of clients to remain economically viable, so they too must be in regular contact with current and potential clientele.

EPA, corporations and trade associations, and other executive branch agencies have low levels of outreach, making only slightly more than half of all contacts. Each of these organizations has substantial scientific and technological capabilities, and each also has the resources to acquire more assistance when necessary. Thus, these institutions do not need to spend as much effort communicating and building policy networks.

The column on the far right of Table 5 is a popularity or *prominence* rating. This percentage is the average across organization groups of the proportion of times an organization group was chosen by our respondents. As in the calculation of outreach, the percentage of members of an organization group contacting other members of the same group was excluded. Note that this prominence score gives the same weight to choice by organization groups with many respondents in our sample, such as EPA, and to groups with few respondents, such as labor and state and local governments. Since our concern in this chapter is with organizations, this equal weight for all types seems more appropriate than a prominence score based on the percentage of respondents saying they talk to a particular organization.

EPA, other executive branch agencies, and corporations and trade associations are the most frequently contacted groups in the community. Each has a prominence score over 75 percent. We believe this is a good indicator of their power. Executive bureaucracies, such as the FDA or the Nuclear Regulatory Commission, are the key actors in "science regulation." For risk professionals to have any influence, they must maintain contact with these "techno-science" agencies and with the political appointees and civil servants who inhabit them.

Corporations and trade associations, while not involved in the making of public policy in the narrow sense, wield great influence in Washington. It is critically important to know their policy positions to operate effectively in the policy arena. This is particularly the case in the Reagan administration, where corporate access to and impact on the policy process has dramatically increased and where environmental health and safety risk reduction measures are highly controversial. This is especially the case for those corporations who view risk control as a central concern in matters such as productivity and competitiveness, and thus are very active in the policy system.[110]

Congress, law and consulting firms, and environmental organizations rank next in prominence, followed by the labor and state and local government grouping. The relatively low profile of Congress is somewhat surprising, because most observers credit the legislative branch with resisting the Reagan effort to dismantle environmental laws and agencies.[111] Part of the explanation may be that the pressure exerted by the Reagan forces, particularly in their first term in office, forced the Congress to move from the more aggressive, proactive stance it had developed in the decade of the 1970s to one essentially defensive and reactive in its attempts to protect legislative and administrative capabilities already in place.[112]

Labor and state and local governments are reactive in their posture. Earlier we noted the strong proenvironmental positions of some labor unions, but a number of analysts have noted the conservative approach of most unions to issues with a high scientific and technological content. While unions are active in the policy system and have substantial influence on some issues, their role is not central. The reactive position of state and local governments can be explained by the recent cuts in support for state environmental programs, such as reductions in grants-in-aid. Decreases in intergovernmental exchanges of personnel have exacerbated this situation.[113]

Finally, the low prominence of universities and think tanks may be an unfortunate artifact of methods. We began by asking respondents which organizations they talk to in a typical month, then asked specifically whether they talked with each of seventeen organizations and organization groups if those institutions had not been mentioned in the general response. These probes, unfortunately, did not include universities or think tanks. As a consequence, the percent of respondents indicating they talk to such bodies may be biased downward. Nonetheless, the very low frequency with which these organizations were mentioned suggests that they are not as central to the environmental health and safety policy process.

The third dimension of personal contact displayed in Table 5 is that of *communication structure*. The diagonal cells of the table represent communication within an organizational group. For EPA this figure represents communication across offices; for other groupings it represents communication with different organizations within the same group. Thus, as we have noted, every respondent at the agency communicates on a regular basis with other EPA offices. Communication within organization groups is very high, reflecting the need to share information, build coalitions, and coordinate activities. The major exceptions are state and local governments, unions, and consulting and law firms. Legal and consulting firms are often competitors, so their need to communicate with each other is minimal. Labor and state and local governments are a rather disparate group of institutions that have been lumped together for analytical convenience. There is a reasonable degree of communication among labor unions, but very little among state and local governments and their representatives or between state and local governments and labor organizations.

Looking at the interior of Table 5, the patterns of communication reflect the roles played by the organization groups. EPA staff are most likely to talk with other federal agencies, and they speak to corporations and environmental groups with equal probability. Law and consulting firms are mentioned next most often by EPA employees, possibly to call upon their analytical services or to discuss matters related to clients regulated by the agency. Sixty percent of EPA respondents report regular communication with Congress, but there is relatively little interaction with labor, state and local governments, and universities or think tanks.

The pattern for other federal agencies is nearly identical, with one major exception. Seventy-one percent of EPA respondents say they talk with trade associations and corporations, and the same percentage reports that they communicate with environmental organizations. Seventy-two percent of our respondents based in other federal agencies report communication with trade associations and corporations, but only 45 percent say they talk to environmental groups. This is not surprising, since environmentalists are a major client of EPA, while other bureaucratic missions focus less directly on environmental concerns. Moreover, other federal agencies were created long before the rise of environmentalism in the late 1960s and early 1970s. As a consequence, environmentalists have not been as important to the federal bureaucracy as they have been to EPA itself.

Congressional and staff support organizations are most likely to talk with federal agencies other than EPA, and somewhat less prone to interact with corporations and trade associations, environmental groups, and EPA. The difference in reported contacts between EPA and other federal agencies is a result of treating EPA as a special case in our analysis. In fact, EPA is contacted more frequently than any other federal agency, but not quite as often as the aggregate of all other federal bureaucracies. Since environmental and corporate interests are the major contenders in environmental policy conflicts, it is not surprising that they are frequently contacted by congressional support organizations and staff.

Every environmental organization employee interviewed reported frequent interaction with Congress. This is consistent with our argument that these groups, with limited funding and personnel but with broad-based public support as the major source of power, must focus on the legislative branch. In environmental policy, as in other areas, Congress generally focuses on broad agenda-setting or formulation issues, leaving detailed implementation to the executive branch agencies.[114] With limited staff, environmental groups target broad concerns rather than details.

And, as noted in previous chapters, there are many ideological and demographic similarities between risk professionals working in Congress and those working in environmental groups.

Law and consulting firms are most likely to have contact with EPA, other federal agencies, and corporations and trade associations. These groups have the resources to make use of outside expertise, and they are the key actors in regulatory proceedings in which high levels of technical and legal expertise are used. The communication pattern for law and consulting firms thus reflects their clientele base and the bodies with which they must negotiate.

In order to understand the structure of the network of risk professionals, we applied cluster analysis to the data in Table 5. This technique groups organizations according to the similarity of their communication patterns.[115] Organizations that play the same role in the network are placed in the same cluster. Two clusters emerge from this analysis. The largest is composed of EPA, other federal agencies, and corporations and trade associations. These groups are actively sought by other organization groups and make substantial outreach efforts themselves. The average level of communication within the cluster, excluding communication within a group, is 77 percent, indicating a high level of within-cluster contact. The second cluster is composed of congressional staff and support organizations and environmental groups. These bodies have made strong outreach efforts, are not as often contacted by other groups, and have an even higher level of communication with each other than was the case with the first cluster. Here the average contact is 88 percent.

Personnel Flows

Personnel flows across organizations also can be an important component of an exchange network. This is a more subtle form of communication, but one of great importance in the Washington policy environment. The phenomenon of the "revolving door" is well known among government bureaucracies, their clientele, and congressional staffs, but an equally important pattern is the "inner-outer" career path, in which individuals move from universities, think tanks, and other organizations into positions in government.[116]

Table 6 displays the percent of respondents working in an organizational group who have ever been employed by each of the other organizational groupings. The diagonal of the matrix represents previous experience in the same grouping, but in a different specific organization, or, in the case of EPA, in a different office.

Over 40 percent of our respondents at EPA have worked at other federal agencies, and an identical percentage have experience at universities and think tanks. When EPA was founded in 1970, it consolidated some 6,000 employees from fifteen government agencies located in three departments (Health, Education and Welfare; Agriculture; and Interior) and in the years that followed it recruited heavily from the rest of the federal bureaucracy.[117] This may help account for EPA respondents' broad experience in the executive branch. Since our respondents are highly educated, and since many EPA employees are engaged in performing highly technical analyses or translating the results of such analysis into policy, it is also not surprising that a large fraction of our respondents there have work experience at universities and think tanks. Unexpected is the fact that over one-quarter of EPA respondents have worked at corporations or trade associations. This is the largest fraction of corporate experience for any of our organizational groupings. A little more than one-tenth of EPA respondents have worked in the legislative branch, and less than 3 percent have any work experience with environmental groups or law and consulting firms. For an agency that was accused of being captured by proenvironmental interests in its early days, the low level of personnel flows from environmental groups is a great surprise. One explanation might be that the erosion of agency morale and budget and personnel cutbacks that took place under Administrator Burford simply drove many former environmentalists out of EPA. Almost as unanticipated is the relative lack of congressional background, especially since experience on "The Hill" seems to be valued among the risk professionals. Not at all surprising is the low level of personnel flow from law and consulting firms to EPA. The high salaries and perquisites of many of these firms, plus the fact that EPA has had "more work per worker" than any other agency, are only two factors that might contribute to the minimal personnel link between these organizations.[118]

The employment patterns of respondents at other executive

Table 6 Patterns of Personnel Flows Among Risk Policy System Organizations

Current Employer	Percent of Respondents with Previous Experience at Other Organizations									
	EPA	Other Executive Agencies	Universities, Think Tanks, NAS/NRC	Congress	Law and Consulting Firms	Environmental Groups	Corporate and Trade Associations	Other	Density
EPA	20.0	42.9	42.9	11.4	2.9	2.9	28.6	80.0	21.9
Other Executive Agencies	20.7	37.9	37.9	3.4	10.3	3.4	17.2	89.7	15.5
Universities, Think Tanks, NAS/NRC	9.5	42.9	38.1	14.3	4.8	9.5	9.5	85.7	15.1
Congress	4.0	36.0	20.0	20.0	20.0	0.0	12.0	88.0	15.3
Law and Consulting Firms	15.2	60.6	30.3	18.2	33.3	9.1	18.2	84.8	25.3
Environmental Groups	11.1	40.7	25.9	7.4	29.6	48.1	0.0	85.2	19.1
Corporations and Trade Associations	15.4	17.9	23.1	12.8	28.2	2.6	51.3	82.1	16.7
Other	5.3	10.5	36.8	5.3	5.3	0.0	5.3	94.7	—
Permeation	11.6	35.9	31.0	10.4	14.4	3.9	13.0	—	—

branch agencies closely parallels that of EPA. The major difference is that fewer respondents in those organizations have corporate experience, while more have worked in consulting or legal firms. Risk professionals currently working at universities and think tanks are most likely to have experience at executive branch agencies other than EPA, and are about equally likely to have worked at all other organizational groupings.

Over one-third of congressional staff or support personnel have experience in non-EPA executive agencies, one-fifth have worked at law or consulting firms, or universities and think tanks, and one-eighth have held positions in the corporate sector. Only 4 percent have had jobs at EPA, while none have ever worked for environmental groups. The lack of experience at EPA seems somewhat unusual, but the absence of prior employment in environmental organizations is absolutely startling, since influencing the legislative branch is a major strategy for environmentalists and, as noted above, environmental and congressional representatives have strong similarities in communication and expertise patterns.

Over 60 percent of law and consulting firm employees have worked at executive agencies other than EPA. This is the highest figure in Table 6. This would appear to be a classic example of the revolving door in federal government. Consultants and attorneys typically have strong personal ties with clients, and often individuals from agencies, or from universities or think tanks, "go private" to establish new businesses or to join existing firms. These individuals rely on their intimate knowledge of the clients' organization and concerns and on the trust that has developed during employment to create and maintain a steady flow of business.[119] Congress does not make extensive use of private consultants or lawyers, which may account for the fact that less than one-fifth of respondents working for law or "beltway bandit" organizations have held jobs within the legislative branch. The limited experience of this group in the corporate sector is harder to explain, since businesses are the principal clients of the legal and consulting community. It may well be that the economic rewards of the corporate sector are great enough to minimize mobility to consulting firms, where both uncertainty and rewards are very large.

Environmentalists have a broad range of experience, including substantial percentages of employees with experience in all organization groupings except Congress and corporations. The low level of congressional ties among employees of environmental groups is as puzzling as the absence of environmental group background was for legislative branch employees, and for the same reasons. Perhaps the "clout" that comes from working on the Hill makes work with groups active in lobbying unattractive by comparison. The sharp ideological differences between environmental groups and corporate and trade association employees undoubtedly constrain movement between these bodies. This is shown by the fact that *none* of our environmental group respondents has ever been employed by corporations, and only 2.6 percent of corporate and trade association employees have ever worked in an environmental organization. It is interesting to note that both environmental groups and corporations and trade associations have high rates of internal mobility, with 48 and 56 percent of respondents, respectively, having been employed elsewhere in the group.

The last column of Table 6 presents a measure of the *diversity* of the job experience of respondents from each organizational grouping. We calculated it by taking the average of all entries in a row, except those for intragroup mobility and for the "other" category. As expected, respondents in law and consulting firms have the greatest diversity of experiences, most likely reflecting the linkages to a range of clients or previous employers. The next most diverse bodies are EPA and the environmental groups. Among federal agencies, EPA is a relative newcomer. More important, new responsibilities have been added to the agency's mandate on a regular basis. From original responsibility for air and water quality under a fairly limited set of statutes, the EPA's charge has grown remarkably. Until recently, this had been accompanied by an expansion of staff, particularly in response to the risk-related issues of concern to our respondents. Presumably, new staff with the requisite skills drawn from a variety of other organization groups leads to the high diversity of experience at EPA. The moderate diversity of employment experience at environmental organizations could be traced to two factors. First, like EPA, the scope of concerns addressed by environmental groups has broadened considerably in the last decade.[120] Second, the Reagan administration has dramatically reduced staffing levels at most federal agencies with environmental health and safety functions. Some of the people who have left the bureaucracy may have joined environmental groups.

The bottom row of Table 6 is a *permeation* index, calculated by averaging all the entries in each column except the diagonal entry. This index measures the ability of an organization group to place its employees in other groupings. As discussed earlier, this is one form of influence that organizations can have on each other. Executive agencies other than EPA and universities and think tanks have the greatest ability to exert this type of influence. These are the two groups with the longest experience with formal risk analysis and risk management issues, so it is reasonable that they can place their former employees quite broadly.

The other organization groups have roughly equivalent permeation indices, with the notable exception of environmental groups. In Chapter 2, while analyzing the career paths of the risk professionals, we observed that working for an environmental group led to a very low probability of finding employment with any other organizational group. The analysis presented in Table 6 indicates that this effect is even stronger here. Individuals with environmental group experience are unlikely to be found anywhere else. Part of this pattern may be a consequence of self-selection. Chapters 3 and 4 demonstrated that members of environmental groups hold values that are somewhat different from those of most other risk professionals, and that they view the policy process very differently. Such values and attitudes may be a large part of the reason these people are willing to work in organizations characterized by limited support resources, fiscal rewards, and the like. The same values, however, may make it difficult to move to other environmental health and safety organizations. Employment at an environmental group may also carry something of a stigma, at least during the Reagan administration's tenure in office, which limits mobility. Finally, environmental groups do not have many workers trained in the natural sciences and engineering and so may simply have few individuals who are attractive for the more technically oriented organizational groupings.

Legitimacy

In addition to flows of communication and personnel, significant linkages among organizations may be facilitated by mutual perceptions. Employees of each of the organizational groups have attitudes and beliefs about each other, and these may shape tactics and strategies on particular issues. Moreover, they may affect the kinds of actions that are seen as fair and effective. Legitimacy is a key issue in any policy arena, and it is especially problematic in environmental policy.[121] As we have discussed in the introductory chapter, environmental problems raise difficult questions about the social costs of private production decisions. Attribution of causes of environmental problems and proposals to resolve them revolve around the issue of governmental intervention in private activities and the ability of market forces to protect the health and safety of members of the society. In general, environmentalists and corporate representatives are at political loggerheads in this debate.

How does the problem of legitimacy manifest itself among our respondents? Most theoretical treatments of legitimacy are highly abstract, focusing on the legitimacy of the overall political system or major components of that system as perceived by the general public. We focus instead on the degree of sympathy our respondents exhibit for the major contenders in the ongoing debates: the environmental movement, corporations, and labor. Thus, our analysis of legitimacy is at a very specific, micro-level. We believe it is from strains at this level that larger crises in legitimacy develop. Lack of sympathy for a particular group's policy position may lead to a lack of sympathy for the legitimacy of the group's suggested remedies, or to the rejection of its qualifications to participate in the system at all. When such cleavages develop in multiple policy arenas, the problem of legitimacy may become systemic. It is this general level that has caught the attention of most theorists.[122]

We have already seen that most risk professionals adopt environmental values to some degree, but that environmental groups are at odds with most other members of the system with regard to their views of the policy process. These patterns could lead to either high or low legitimacy for major actors in the system.

To gauge how our respondents rate the legitimacy of groups, we asked them if they were "very sympathetic," "somewhat sympathetic," or "not at all sympathetic" to industry, the environmental movement, and labor. We did not ask about other organizational groups because, at least from our vantage point, government, consultants and lawyers, universities, etcetera, do not hold general positions on policy that are consistent over time, but rather comprise a range of stances. To put it differently, labor, environmental groups, and corporations tend to make broad appeals to all other participants for support on issues. When other actors make such appeals, as in the case of state and local governments calling for more autonomy, or academics asking for more research funding, their arguments tend to be seen as neutral, and are less likely to raise issues of legitimacy.

Table 7 displays the percentage of respondents from each organizational group who say that they are somewhat or very sympathetic with industry, labor, and environmentalists. The overall level of sympathy is high, with nearly three-quarters of respondents expressing some sympathy with industry, four-fifths showing some sympathy with labor, and 96 percent expressing sympathy with the environmental movement. However, there are some important variations in the overall pattern of legitimacy. First, the proportion of respondents saying they have some sympathy with industry is lower than the percent saying they have some sympathy with environmental groups for every group of organizations except corporations and trade associations. For "very sympathetic" responses the difference is dramatic. Organized labor is also accorded more legitimacy than industry by every organizational group except corporations and trade associations and universities and think tanks.

Do the major contenders view each other with sympathy? No respondent from environmental groups or labor organizations considered himself or herself very sympathetic with industry, and less than half expressed any sympathy with industrial organizations. In contrast, nearly 90 percent of corporation and trade association employees expressed some sympathy with the environmental movement, and over three-quarters said the same thing about labor groups. All employees in labor organizations and state and local government had some sympathy with the environmental movement, and 96 percent of environmental group members had some sympathy with labor.

It appears that while the overall level of legitimacy is quite high, industry is not viewed as sympathetically as are the environmentalists or labor organizations. The lower level of sympathy for industry expressed by environmental organizations, labor, and state and local governments suggests some strains in the legitimacy of the policy system. Perhaps this is because the industrial reaction to environmental health and safety has followed a pattern increasingly seen by some actors as counter to the public in-

Table 7 Percent of Respondents Employed by Each Organization Indicating Sympathy with Industry, Environmental Groups, and Labor

	EPA	Other Executive Agencies	Congress	Environmental Groups	Corporate and Trade Associations	Law and Consulting Firms	Universities, Think Tanks, NAS/NRC	Labor, State and Local Government	Overall
SYMPATHY WITH INDUSTRY									
"Very" or "Somewhat" Sympathetic	76.4	77.8	79.2	40.7	94.8	65.7	90.5	44.4	73.0
"Very" Sympathetic	8.8	0.0	4.2	0.0	33.3	6.3	14.3	0.0	9.9
SYMPATHY WITH ENVIRONMENTAL MOVEMENT									
"Very" or "Somewhat" Sympathetic	100.0	96.3	100.0	100.0	87.5	97.0	95.2	100.0	96.5
"Very" Sympathetic	47.1	29.6	44.0	85.2	10.0	18.2	33.3	55.6	37.8
SYMPATHY WITH LABOR									
"Very" or "Somewhat" Sympathetic	87.9	88.4	80.0	96.3	77.5	75.0	66.6	94.2	82.8
"Very" Sympathetic	21.2	26.9	12.0	18.5	7.5	21.9	9.5	47.1	19.0

NOTE: 222 respondents answered the questions about industry and labor, while 225 answered the question about the environmental movement.

terest. As we have noted, this pattern typically takes the form of industrial denial of the existence or severity of specific environmental problems when they are raised by workers or environmentalists. If sufficient political pressure is brought to bear and regulation is proposed, then industry will tend to argue for further analysis, or suggest minimal intervention or some form of mitigation subsidy. Once controls are in effect, industrial interests suffer some divisions in their ranks, as government regulation creates new special interests, some of which are beneficiaries of the new rules. However, the cost-bearers of regulation can be expected to be a constant force pressing for deregulation. This is a predictable set of interest group reactions intended to affect the distribution of costs and benefits.[123] But debate after debate places industry in the position of denying the need for change until the pressure is overwhelming. The need to keep private costs of production as low as possible by minimizing environmental protection flies in the face of public concern. This behavior is amplified by the occasional, well-publicized case of flagrant violations of environmental regulations by industry.[124] The consequence is a very limited legitimacy for industry among its antagonists in environmental politics, including workers.[125] And the same process, rather than portraying environmentalists and labor as "doomsayers," seems to enhance their credibility as they remain relatively free from major scandals and promote positions seen as in the public rather than the private interest.

Power

A natural complement to legitimacy is power. Legitimacy is the essential condition for effective authority; indeed, authority can be defined as legitimized power. The environmental groups and labor are seen as legitimate by all organizational groupings in our study, while industry has low legitimacy with its antagonists but reasonably high levels elsewhere. Are these differences in sympathy paralleled by perceived differences in power?

Table 8 shows the perceived influence of industry, the environmental movement, and labor as viewed by respondents in each of the eight organizational groupings. Overall, all three sets of actors are seen as having some influence, but while a majority of respondents said industry and the environmental groups are very

Table 8 Influence of Industry, Environmental Groups, and Labor as Viewed by Respondents Employed in Each Organization

	EPA	Other Executive Agencies	Congress	Environmental Groups	Corporate and Trade Associations	Law and Consulting Firms	Universities, Think Tanks, NAS/NRC	Labor, State and Local Government	Overall
INFLUENCE OF INDUSTRY									
"Very" or "Somewhat" Influential	100.0	100.0	96.0	100.0	92.5	90.9	100.0	100.0	96.9
"Very" Influential	68.6	82.8	80.0	92.6	20.0	57.6	71.4	72.8	64.9
INFLUENCE OF ENVIRONMENTAL MOVEMENT									
"Very" or "Somewhat" Influential	97.2	93.1	96.0	100.0	100.0	100.0	95.2	100.0	97.8
"Very" Influential	48.6	48.3	44.0	44.4	72.5	63.6	61.9	50.0	55.3
INFLUENCE OF LABOR									
"Very" or "Somewhat" Influential	52.9	66.7	75.0	85.2	80.0	65.6	66.7	94.1	72.1
"Very" Influential	2.9	11.1	25.0	11.1	30.0	12.5	4.8	0.0	13.5

NOTE: 221 respondents answered the question regarding industry, 223 the question regarding labor, and 223 the question regarding the environmental movement.

influential, only about 14 percent said the same thing about labor. This is consistent with our finding that labor organizations have a very limited presence in environmental health and safety risk policy.

Industry is seen as being very influential by a majority of respondents employed in every organizational group except their own. Only one-fifth of employees of corporations and trade associations considered these bodies to be very influential. This "organizational humility" is also displayed by labor and environmental groups. Indeed, no one working for labor or state and local governments thought labor was very influential.

In general, the environmental movement is seen as less influential than industry. Corporations and trade associations and law and consulting firms are the only exceptions to this rule. Trade associations and corporations attribute great influence to their antagonists, with nearly three-quarters of those respondents saying that the environmental movement is very influential. Law and consulting firm employees are only slightly more likely to attribute power to industry. Congress, EPA, and other executive agencies do not share this view. They are substantially more likely to respond that industry is very influential than to attribute such influence to the environmental movement.

Associating minimal influence with one's own organization and great power with one's opponent is a rational strategy that allows an interest to take credit for its victories but be free from blame for failures. It is also a mechanism for gaining sympathy and legitimacy. But it may also become a self-fulfilling prophecy, with those parties-at-interest that are assumed to be powerful eventually acquiring influence by their reputation. The organizations being influenced have quite consistent views regarding the three actor categories we have examined, with the single discrepancy that Congress tends to attribute more influence to labor than to EPA or other executive agencies. It seems that while the environmental movement and labor have more legitimacy, their more limited resources and smaller numbers of risk professionals make it difficult for them to translate that legitimacy into power, while industrial organizations remain powerful in the environmental health and safety arena even if they are not considered as legitimate.

Conclusion

One notable feature of the network structure of the risk policy community is the position of the environmental organizations. They are viewed quite sympathetically by the rest of the organizational groupings, and are seen as influential, though not as influential as their antagonists. They make substantial efforts to contact others but are not a particularly attractive contact themselves. And their place in the network of personnel flows is marginal, with very few former environmental group members finding employment in other parts of the risk profession.

In contrast, corporations and trade associations are viewed with much less sympathy but are seen as much more influential. They are frequently contacted, but they make fewer outreach efforts themselves. And while former corporate employees are more common throughout the network than former environmentalists, they are still less common than individuals with experience in the federal government or in law and consulting firms.

Two factors may help explain the structure of these networks. The first is whether or not an organization is a policy advocate. Employment at environmental groups or corporations and trade associations appears to involve substantial commitment to specific positions on policy issues. As we noted in Chapter 4, corporations and environmental groups are at opposite ends of the policy spectrum with regard to their level of optimism about the utility of cost-benefit and risk analysis and sources of and responses to scientific controversies. And in Chapter 3 we documented the ideological differences between the groups. Once groups embrace an ideology, it may be difficult to move to more neutral positions or more neutral organizations.

Flows of communication may relate to a second factor, the character of the organization itself. Factors such as the level of in-house expertise might account for patterns of interaction across our organizational groupings. EPA, other executive agencies, and corporations and trade associations thus might have fewer incentives to talk to other actors, while Congress and environmental groups face the reverse situation.

Differences in perceived legitimacy of environmentalists and industry may be connected to positions on policy issues as well, but a stronger link would seem to be attitudes toward environmentalism. Our analysis of this dimension in Chapter 3 demonstrated that our respondents tend to hold proenvironment values, so sympathy with the environmental groups is hardly surprising.

Many parts of this analysis suggest that the risk policy system functions as a policy community. Overall levels of personal contact are high, with almost two-thirds of all possible communications being manifested in the analysis. And there are linkages among every major component of the risk profession, indicating that a network does in fact exist.

Knoke and Laumann suggest that attentiveness to policy is the key factor in the creation and maintenance of a policy network.[126] We concur that attentiveness defines a policy system, but we have tried to elucidate the structure of the system as well as demonstrate its existence. Our analysis has shown the network of risk professionals is very dense, and the most comprehensive communications linkages are maintained, as theory would suggest, by environmental groups. These groups reach out to potential adversaries almost as often as potential coalition partners. This is consistent with the notion that "skill in using these networks is a prerequisite for success in influencing policy" and that "on the whole, environmentalists have been successful in developing and using these networks."[127]

Here, as in our examinations based on elite, class, and establishment perspectives, we have found a number of general characteristics of risk professionals. Equally important, we have found substantial and systematic differences across types of actors in the risk policy system. In the final chapter, we develop a picture of risk professionals that integrates our findings and relates them to general problems in environmental policy.

Chapter 6 Conclusions

In his 1984 presidential address to the American Sociological Association, James F. Short, Jr., urged a "social transformation of risk analysis." He argued that "risk analysis has insisted on its own legitimacy and pressed for policies based on technical analyses, while failing to acknowledge the narrow focus and tenuous quality of those analyses and ignoring the consequences of failed expertise."[128] The transformation he had in mind was nothing less than the demystification of risk analysis by embedding it in a broader social context.

One of the goals of this study is just such a demystification. It is our hope that by developing a better understanding of the risk policy system and of the risk professionals who work in that system, we will come to a better understanding of how modern industrial societies attempt to deal with environmental and technological hazards. In order to make sense of our work, we must make our understanding of the risk professionals part of a broader examination of the social structure and dynamics that influence environmental health and safety policy in the United States. The constraints of the larger political and economic system have important consequences for the risk policy system, and by coming to grips with them we can interpret the findings of previous chapters. Thus, we begin this final chapter by considering the relationship between the risk policy system, including the professionals who are the focal point of our work, and the political economy of environmental health and safety problems in American society. After examining those links, we draw some general conclusions about the risk policy system. Finally, we offer some tentative suggestions about ways in which the risk policy system might be improved.

Public Opinion, the Environmental Movement, and the Risk Policy System

The risk policy system in its present form is relatively new. It grew out of a history of political conflict over environmental issues and continues to reflect that conflict. A confluence of events in the late 1960s and early 1970s produced both the modern environmental movement and broad public support for environmental programs. Throughout the 1960s, scientific evidence accumulated on a number of threats to human health and safety. Evidence of the serious consequences of water pollution, air pollution, and pesticide use mounted rapidly. While studies of environmental problems are as old as concern with public health, the post-World War II developments in ecology and environmental science produced a body of evidence that indicated that environmental problems were more prevalent and more serious than had been suspected.

This research mobilized concern among a group of activists who were to form the core of the environmental movement. The United States had a long history of concern with conservation, and some of that concern translated into an awareness of air and water pollution problems and of toxic substances in general. But during the late 1960s, a number of individuals who had been active in the civil rights and anti-Vietnam War movements and who were participating in the emergence of the second wave of the feminist movement became involved in environmental issues. While in the past members of the conservation movement were usually political moderates who supported the general ideology of growth that we have labeled the dominant social paradigm, the new proponents of environmental reform came from political backgrounds that made them question the legitimacy of the political and economic system. This view caused the new activists to engage in broader critiques than had been typical of the conservationists. From their analyses emerged the worldview we have termed the new environmental paradigm.

The new environmental movement drew upon tactics developed by the civil rights and antiwar movements. Whereas the traditional conservationists relied on lobbying efforts, appeals to the common good, and their links to the power elite, the new environmentalists depended on demonstrations and other events staged for the press to attract public attention. A particularly dramatic example of this approach was the environmental teach-in in April 1970 that coordinated demonstrations and activities in hundreds of colleges and communities across the country.

Nearly fifteen years of survey data indicate strong and virtually unwavering support for environmental protection on the part of the American public.[129] In part, this is due to scientific evidence, which continues to point out new and ever more serious hazards. But it also appears that environmental issues tap a fundamental concern among the general public, one that has provided broad political backing for the development of policy to protect the environment. With this success, the environmental movement has been able to move from actions intended to raise public consciousness to work within the policy system. However, as we have noted in previous chapters, within the policy system environmentalists often face active opposition from corporate interests who find environmental regulation a serious threat.

Scientific knowledge about environmental problems, strong public support for environmental protection, the evolution of the environmental movement itself, and the character of opposition to that movement form the political and economic context within which the risk policy system is embedded. Four resources are critical to successful action. First, because science is the basis for understanding environmental problems, actors in the system must maintain involvement in the system. Second, the basic positions taken by an actor must be seen as legitimate by other actors in the policy system. Third, actors must have the material resources to be able to maintain participation in the system; funding, personnel, and the like must be available in sufficient amounts to enable an ongoing involvement. And fourth, actors must have public support for their involvement if they are to enhance their political agenda. Some of these resources, particularly funding and public support, depend critically on the links between the risk policy system and the rest of society, and it is through these links that the broader social context influences risk policy. Other resources, especially legitimacy and credibility, are internal to the system and depend critically on an actor's history. By taking account of both the exogenous and endogenous factors, we believe we can make some sense of the structure and dynamics of the risk policy system.

How does our study help us understand how this policy system works? In the following section, we offer some general conclusions about the functioning of the risk policy system, drawing on the evidence of the previous chapters.

Some General Themes

THE RISK POLICY SYSTEM IS AN OPEN SYSTEM

The four perspectives we used to generate questions about the risk policy system suggest that there may be sharp boundaries to the system, and that entry to it may be limited. Indeed, each of the perspectives suggests factors that may be critical to participating in the system and thus may limit involvement by making the system difficult to enter. In fact, this does not seem to be the case.

When we began this study, we were concerned that a danger establishment, sharing some characteristics of the military establishment, might have developed around environmental health and safety issues. Although there is little consensus among analysts of the military establishment, or the "military-industrial complex," one of the standard definitions describes it as "an informal alliance among key military, governmental and corporate decision makers involved in the highly profitable weapons-procurement and military-support system."[130]

We feel there is little evidence to support this view of the risk policy system. To be sure, the military establishment and environmental health and safety arenas share some important traits. Both have a range of participants, both have a core of professionals, and both involve technical information used to justify or criticize policies that also have significant ideological and political implications. What makes the risk policy system different is the fact that there are clear conflicts between environmental and corporate representatives. It is the conflict between these two groups that drives the system. As expected from new class theory, environmental ideology permeates the risk policy system, but there are clear differences between antagonists on basic ideological questions and perspectives. And when one turns to issues of how the policy process should function, there is even more marked disagreement. Unlike the military establishment, which is characterized by a strong, pervasive optimism about the utility of modern science and technology in resolving policy problems and a fascination with technical analysis and hardware in general,[131] many of our respondents exhibit mixed views on these subjects. One can be an active and influential member of the risk policy system and reject many procedures used in "scientific" risk analysis, for example, even if the consensus view favors such methods.

This lack of consensus about ideology and the appropriate methods for carrying out policy analysis shows that the risk policy system gives legitimacy to a range of positions. Nor does our evidence on communication and legitimacy across organizations suggest that some parts of the system are marginal. Indeed, we suspect that the risk policy system is relatively easy for a new professional or organization to enter. Both the dominant social paradigm and the new environmental paradigm have significant support within the community and with the general public, so positions consistent with either will have some degree of internal and external legitimacy. A potential participant would, of course, need a material resource base to allow ongoing activity within the system. And scientific legitimacy within the system would come either with preestablished credentials or with the demonstration of competence through ongoing involvement in the system. This suggests that entry would not be difficult and that the risk policy system has not evolved into the static and stable circle of actors, an "old boy" system, that may typify many policy systems.[132]

THE HYBRID CHARACTER OF THE RISK POLICY SYSTEM CREATES CONTRADICTIONS FOR PARTICIPANTS

The risk policy system is a "hybrid" in the sense that it deals with policy issues that have a strong base in science but that also involve sharp ideological differences between participants. As we have noted, actors in the system must maintain scientific credibility while at the same time retaining political support outside the system. The first requirement leads to what Hugh Heclo has referred to as "policy as an intramural activity," in which highly knowledgeable policy experts emerge. He calls these experts "policy politicians—experts in using experts, victuallers of knowledge in a world hungry for right decisions."[133] But these concerns for scientific and technical credibility create strains with the sources of political support for the participants. This is what Peter Weingart terms a hybrid system:

> the institutional expression of the increased communication pressures between the differentiated systems of politics, science, and the economy. Their function is to help define policy problems in terms of systematic knowledge, to translate (operationalize) them into technical goals, to turn them into research, strategies, development programmes and correlate policy measures, all of which feed back into the perception and definition of the policy problems themselves. The significance of the "hybrid communities," therefore, lies in their cognitive function as brokers of expert knowledge and political values.[134]

The internal dynamics of the risk policy system require that action be justified in scientific terms. But the need for political support outside the system depends not on technical justifications, the cost-benefit ratios and risk assessments, but on appeals consistent with the ideologies relevant to environmental problems in the larger society, the new environmental paradigm and the dominant social paradigm. These tensions are the most acute for the environmental movement.

By the late 1970s, a number of observers of environmental organizations were calling for fundamental changes in the movement, and especially for a reassessment of perceived elitist and antiscientific strains characteristic of some elements of environmental groups.[135] These critics suggested that the movement required dramatic changes in orientation, particularly in the area of greater institutional capabilities, which would increase policy effectiveness. Thus, Langton has identified five "new competencies" the movement needs to develop to respond to the increasing complexities of environmental policy: higher levels of professional administrative skills; greater intra- and intermovement collaboration across organizational boundaries; upgraded political action (legislative development, and so on); expanded scientific and technical expertise; and more pragmatic efforts to educate the public and communicate with other actors.[136] Success in placing environmental issues on the national policy agenda has forced environmentalists to become more concerned with the details of policy, which requires different tactics than those used in the early days of the movement. Attempts to move in these directions in recent years have altered the nature of the movement. A recent assessment of the movement's evolution in the 1980s painted a picture of environmental groups being led by "pragmatic managers" reaching out to form new coalitions to solve problems "requiring more professional expertise" through a "less aggressive posture."[137]

The evidence reported in Chapter 2 indicates that environmental organizations remain distinct from other actors in the policy system, but there can be no doubt that many movement groups have been moving toward professionalism. These changes are not without cost. As noted in Chapter 3, some critics claim that Washington-based environmental organizations have sold out, that the day-to-day pressures of participating in the policy system have caused them to lose sight of their original purpose and to lose their critical perspective.[138] Indeed, the contrast between the requirements of scientific credibility within the system and the requisite to maintain broad political support, and especially links with the "grassroots," has led to a protracted and contentious battle for control of Friends of the Earth (FOE), one of the prototypical new environmental groups to emerge during the late 1960s. The conflict within FOE was largely about whether the organization should move its headquarters from San Francisco to Washington, D.C., and cut back on regional offices and activities in order to maintain a strong lobbying presence.[139]

Such conflicts cannot be resolved easily. To influence policy, environmentalists must be effective participants in the risk policy system, and thus use the resources that are intrinsic to the system. But if they lend full credence to rational policy analysis methods and total reliance on current science, they can be overwhelmed by the greater technical resources of their opponents. And environmental groups depend on mass appeals for both material resources and political support. If they move too close to their opponents in the system, if they adopt common policy positions and a "Washington danger establishment" resembling the military establishment does emerge, environmentalists could lose the base of support that has been critical to their very existence.

Corporate representatives face a somewhat different problem. As we have observed in Chapter 5, they are not as legitimate within the system nor do they have as much support from the general public. But corporations, being at the core of the production system, can draw upon vast material resources and the general acceptance of the dominant social paradigm to protect their position within the risk policy system. Thus, unlike their environmentalist antagonists, they do not have as difficult a job in balancing appeals within the system with appeals to the general public. As long as corporate representatives can convince their superiors that they are effective in moderating the worst consequences of environmental regulations, they can be reasonably sure of material support. And as long as the current political and economic system retains general legitimacy, they have a basis for their calls to limit interference with the production process. Nevertheless, because their appeals often seem self-interested, they may be viewed with some suspicion by the general public and by many risk professionals.

SCIENCE IS CENTRAL TO THE RISK POLICY SYSTEM, BUT MANY RISK POLICY PROBLEMS ARE TRANSSCIENTIFIC

Environmental health and safety problems can be understood only in a scientific context. In addition, the complexity of risk policy leads many, but by no means all, participants in the risk policy system to advocate the use of scientific methods of policy analysis such as cost-benefit analysis and formal risk analysis to clarify problems and to suggest preferred policy options. As we have said, this means that all actors must have some scientific credibility to perform effectively.

The science of the risk policy system is a problem-oriented science, intended to provide information of utility for making policy decisions. Wesley Schrum has described the character of such science with reference to cancer research and plasma physics:

> The distinction between basic and applied science breaks down in fields such as cancer research and plasma physics where political needs require such complex developments that new fundamental knowledge is required before successful applications can result. The solution of specific social, economic, and military problems is seen to follow from a series of transformations: social programmes into political programmes, political goals into science policy

programmes, and science policy programmes into concrete research strategies. These transfers are achieved by hybrid communities involving scientists, politicians, civil servants and experts from industry as well as from other interest groups.[140]

During the 1960s and 1970s the federal government attempted to mobilize science to solve urgent national problems, such as those of health, the environment, and energy. Many observers feel that this period constituted a new era in American science. Some are critical of it, viewing it as "defensive," or even "antitechnology."[141] Others view it positively, calling it "purposive," or "democratic."[142] But there is a consensus that the rise of problem-oriented science represents a challenge to the traditional "disconnectedness" of science and politics.

One implication of problem-oriented science is a weakening of disciplinary perspectives and a strengthening of viewpoints based on politics and ideology. Among our respondents, field of education has relatively little effect on attitudes and values, while organizational affiliation has a very strong effect. Once entering the risk policy system, a physicist or biologist has his or her worldview shaped more by the workplace than by a discipline or by training. In policy systems in which there is little ideological diversity, there may be few pressures to counteract disciplinary socialization. But in the risk policy system the differences in ideology and in views of the appropriate ways of conducting the policy process provide strong forces that overwhelm any commonality based on disciplinary affiliation.

The importance of science has important implications for the dynamics of the policy system. And these implications go beyond the obvious advantages that corporate interests have in generating research and analysis to bolster their positions. Alan Schnaiberg has pointed out a further problem with the scientific base for environmental policy. A long tradition of public and private research and development has led to a strong base in what he calls the "production" sciences. These are branches of the natural and social sciences whose application facilitates the activities of the production system. In contrast, the "impact sciences," which serve to document the failures of the production system, are only weakly developed.[143] In fact, though the amount of funds on environmental research has increased greatly during the last twenty years, it still represents a miniscule part of the federal science budget. Paul Ehrlich notes that the annual federal budget for biomedical research is over 100 times larger than the budget for ecological research.[144]

A third problem in the use of science in the risk policy system lies with the social science techniques such as risk analysis and cost-benefit analysis that are advocated as mechanisms for rationalizing the policy process. The theoretical and empirical underpinnings of those techniques reflect the assumptions and research base of the production sciences. It is relatively easy to quantify the economic costs associated with a regulatory strategy, but it is much more difficult to estimate the public and health benefits and translate those into dollar values.

All of these factors make the essential role of science in the risk policy system also a problematic one. Corporate representatives mistrust government science because they often see it used to justify environmentalist positions. Environmentalists distrust research funded by corporations or government and the use of formal analytical techniques because they feel the research may be biased against their interests.

Nor would it be reasonable to expect that better research and data could wholly eliminate this mistrust. To the extent that conflict within the risk policy system reflects differences in basic attitudes and values as well as positions on specific policy issues and the conduct of the policy process, conflict will persist. The risk policy system is clearly a "transscientific" domain. The term was first coined by Alvin Weinberg to describe problems characterized by great uncertainty for which adequate solutions could not be supplied by science alone, and it has been applied to environmental problems for some time. The first example cited by Weinberg was the risks associated with exposure to low levels of radioactivity.[145] Some questions that are central to the risk policy system, such as what constitutes an acceptable level of risk for the general public, are inherently political questions. Second, many techniques of policy analysis require assumptions about the appropriate method for assigning values to policy impacts. Clearly, decisions about the appropriate value to assign to a human life or a scenic vista are as much political as scientific. Third, many empirical and theoretical questions in the environmental and risk sciences may be resolvable in principle but will never be resolved in practice because of the magnitude and complexity of the research required. Finally, the limited resources available for research require difficult choices about research priorities, and those decisions inevitably involve political as well as scientific factors. All of this makes the role of science in the risk policy system inextricable from the role of politics and ideology.

This is not to argue that science is completely reduced to or corrupted by politics. Rather, an understanding of the dynamics of the system suggests that we must understand that science is embedded in politics. Consider two physicists, one Republican, one Democrat, one an adherent of the dominant social paradigm and the other more sympathetic to the new environmental worldview. Both would calculate the same half-lethal dose from a given experiment. But they might differ sharply in their interpretation of the results, and each would assign a different priority to future research on the impact of production of the compound. It is at this level that science and politics are intertwined. In this regard, problem-oriented science may not differ significantly from "pure" science. Karen Knorr-Cetina discusses the importance of "networks of symbolic relationships which in principle go beyond the boundaries of a scientific community or scientific field." Her descriptions of these networks suggest the importance of the internal political dynamics of pure science in determining scientific production.[146] The difference between pure science and the science of the risk policy system is only that the latter is more obviously embedded in the politics of the system and of the larger society.

Implications for Environmental Policy

We began this study as an effort to reach a better understanding of the risk policy system and of the risk professionals who inhabit it. Our orientation is that of natural historians as much as policy scientists. But one does not engage in the study of a policy system without some interest in the policies that are the focus of that system. Thus, we offer a few suggestions about the implications of our work for environmental health and safety policy.

First, to paraphrase James Wilson's observation about regulatory politics, a single-explanation theory of environmental health and safety policy is about as helpful as a single explanation of politics generally.[147] While each of the perspectives we use in this analysis generates useful questions and provides some insight about risk professionals, none constitutes a theory or an adequate description of the risk policy system. Discussions of the system that are to be satisfactory must take into account its evolution and its ongoing internal dynamics, as well as its linkages to the larger political and economic system. Analyses that focus on only one set of actors or that consider the policy system in isolation are likely to be misleading.

Second, analyses of risk policy should consider the importance of the natural as well as the social world. Environmental policy systems are driven by physical facts as much as by social ones, yet there is some bias against considering physical facts in much social analysis.[148] Dramatic discoveries and accidents place pressures on the risk policy system, and the system is constrained by what is physically possible as well as what is socially and politically feasible. It is the critical importance of the natural world that makes expertise the focal point of the risk policy system.[149] This is not to say that accidents such as Chernobyl or Three Mile Island do not have social causes, or acquire social meanings—become "normal," in Charles Perrow's terms.[150] But the dynamics of such policy systems do not reduce to the social. Any approach to risk policy that minimizes the importance of physical facts by overemphasizing the cultural, for example, are likely to be off target.

Third, we are not sanguine about attempts to "rationalize" the risk policy system. We began this book with a discussion of William Ruckelshaus's efforts to separate the science of assessing risks from the policy of managing them. But science is inextricably linked to politics and to the differential resources actors bring to the system. The professionals in the risk policy system perceive it that way. So efforts to disentangle the two are not likely to be successful. Instead, we agree with the assessment provided by Dale Hattis and David Kennedy:

> There is only one problem with this call for authoritative, scientific risk assessment: such a commodity does not exist. In classical times, there was a great demand for the skills of soothsayers in reading entrails, and there is a similar amount of wishful thinking going on today. The fact is that the science behind risk assessment is not up to the challenge of consistently providing accurate answers about the degree of risk individuals or populations face from health hazards. . . . There is no way risk analysts at

the EPA or other agencies can escape making value-laden choices in the course of their work—choices that render their results far less "scientific" and objective than Ruckelshaus envisioned.[151]

Simplistic attempts to streamline or restructure the risk policy system along "rationalistic" lines will lead only to more frustrations and what George Downs and Patrick Larkey call the "mismatch between analysis and politics."[152]

Fourth, while science and politics can never be separate in the risk policy system, more and better science is badly needed. Some of the conflict over science and formal policy analysis is inherent and cannot be eliminated. We believe that more base-line studies, further research on methodologies, retrospective studies of policy impacts, and efforts intended to maintain strong linkages between the problem-oriented science of the policy system and traditional disciplinary science will provide science that is more generally accepted by most risk professionals. The credibility of research would be greatly enhanced if attempts were made to balance the access to research by the parties-at-interest in the risk policy system. In particular, more research conducted by environmentalists and by independent researchers at think tanks and universities seems warranted. Good science will not eliminate controversy, but it will serve to clarify and focus debate on the issues that most require it.

Fifth, efforts to develop methods of policy analysis should begin with the premise that conflict is inherent in the policy system. No policy option is optimal for all parties in the system. This implies that policy analysis methods should focus on specifying areas of conflict and clarifying the bases for disagreements rather than on a search for the best policy alternative. In our survey, risk professionals who supported the use of cost-benefit analysis usually justified it as a mechanism for the clarification of issues and the focusing of debate. But those who were critical of its use emphasized its inherent biases and its use as a conclusionary document. We suggest that policy analysis in the risk policy system should return to the model of impact assessment, in which the intent is to delineate all impacts and to specify the level of certainty associated with each, under the assumption that individuals will differ in the significance they associate with a particular impact. Resolution of these differences is best viewed as a political not a technical problem.[153] We also note that risk professionals are supportive of conflict resolution and mediation efforts. It may be useful to conduct some experiments with such mechanisms. Already there are several reports of success with environmental mediation, but they have been produced by individuals and organizations who have pioneered in its use and do not provide assessments of the typical application.[154]

Finally, we believe there is a need for a better understanding of the links between the risk policy system and the rest of society. Our presentation of these relationships must be viewed as an initial effort. Far more theoretical and empirical work is needed to understand the interplay between policy systems and the larger society, and the coevolution of both. Comparative analyses with other policy systems would be especially useful in the delineation of factors unique to environmental health and safety policy and elements that are shared across systems. Out of such research should come some prescriptions to improve the quality of policy itself, and such understanding would help reduce the adverse impact of modern society on the natural environment.

Appendix A Methodology

In this appendix, we present a brief discussion of the methods used to conduct this study. In particular, we describe the techniques used to sample individuals, the problems encountered in developing a questionnaire for use with a highly knowledgeable group, the way interviews were carried out, and the steps involved in turning the results of our interviews into a form that could be analyzed.

Developing a Sample

The first step in developing a sample is to determine what kinds of people should be interviewed. We considered several approaches. In many surveys, the researcher begins with a sampling frame in the form of a list of the population to be sampled. One possible sampling frame for our study would have been a list of all members of the Society for Risk Analysis (SRA). A random sample could have been drawn from that list, and used as our sample. But our experience in talking with SRA members and with other individuals involved in risk policy issues was that the

SRA, while influential, was composed primarily of people involved in the technical aspects of risk analysis. Many people interested exclusively in risk policy are not members. Thus, we felt a sample drawn from SRA membership lists would tend to underrepresent those people who were engaged more in the political and social aspects of risk assessment and management. Only 14 percent of our sample were members of the SRA.

Another approach would have been to develop a list of all institutions concerned with environmental risk policy, collect tables of organization for each of them, and draw samples of the staff. We anticipated several problems with this method. First, it was not clear how the relevant organizations could be identified in any fashion that would guarantee reasonably exhaustive coverage. Second, obtaining accurate tables of organization or other sources of data and deciding how to sample from them represented a difficult process. Third, the use of a list of organizations required some decisions about how many individuals to sample from within the unit. Analysts often use organizations as their unit of analysis, and so conduct interviews with individuals primarily to develop a profile of institutional characteristics. This is an interesting approach, but we chose the individual, not the organization, as our unit of analysis.

The approach we used was based on our knowledge of risk professionals. For two years before the beginning of this study, we had conducted a series of seminars for the Washington-based environmental science and policy professionals under the sponsorship of the Environmental Protection Agency (EPA). A major product of this series was the development of an invitation list of some 300 names. We had inventoried a variety of directories and conducted numerous interviews with individuals who were knowledgeable about that professional group. Over the course of the seminar series, we became very familiar with the key dimensions of this group, and especially with the individuals who appeared to be central to it.

Using the invitation list, we selected an initial, purposive sample of twenty people using three criteria: (1) active group membership and strong communication linkages; (2) participation in the seminar series and thus likelihood of cooperation with the study; and (3) selection of at least two individuals from each major institutional grouping that we could identify as active in the environmental policy process. Our intent was to use these twenty people as a starting point in developing our sample. We were able to schedule interviews with nineteen of the twenty during the initial phase of the interviewing, though the final person was interviewed at a later point in the study. These interviews had two goals. One was to provide a pretest of the survey instrument. The other was to initiate the sampling procedure itself. Each person interviewed was asked:

> In this study we want to interview people whose professional activities are centered on assessing environmental risks or debating policies intended to avert or mitigate environmental risks. We are interested in individuals in both the public and private sectors. Could you suggest five individuals we might want to interview?

Cooperation with this question was excellent. In most cases, our interviewees provided not only names and institutional affiliations but also phone numbers for the people they nominated. When the interviewer returned to our project offices, this information was entered on a three-by-five card which was then added to the file that constituted the sampling frame for the study. After the initial nineteen interviews, there were approximately ninety-five nominations. When it was necessary to draw new names for subsequent interviews, cards were drawn at random from this file. As interviews were completed, cards were continuously entered for new nominations, and new names were drawn about once a week until we had interviewed 228 individuals. Overall, 733 different risk professionals were nominated. Note that one card was entered for each nomination, so that a particularly prominent person might have a large number of cards in the file. Thus, our sample of the Washington risk profession was one in which an individual's probability of selection in the sample was directly proportional to his or her prominence. Five hundred and thirty-eight people were nominated only once, while two people were nominated nineteen times.

The use of this kind of "snowball" sampling technique corresponded to our concept of the risk profession. As indicated throughout the previous chapters and in the quote above, we define the profession largely in terms of those individuals whose activity centers on assessing or managing risks of an environmental nature. And our experience in Washington suggested that personal contacts were a critical part of both those tasks. We assumed that these professionals would know each other.

We note two weaknesses in this approach. First, the probability that an individual will be in our sample is directly proportional to that person's prominence in the community. We do not believe this builds serious bias into our sample, but rather matches our conception of the policy system. There is a continuum from highly prominent individuals at the core of the risk policy system to those who participate only episodically. We wanted to include all those at the core. We were less interested in occasional participants. Thus, probability proportional to prominence seemed proper for our purposes.

The second problem is that the sampling errors associated with our sample are difficult to determine. We believe we have sampled a large fraction of the population, perhaps 10–25 percent of all risk professionals as we have defined them. If our sample were a simple random sample, techniques used to estimate species frequency distributions could be used to estimate the size of the population, and standard errors could be calculated.[155] But these methods have not been developed for snowball samples. Without a correction based on population size, statistical tests based on a simple random sample, such as the chi-squared test for association in contingency tables, will overestimate sampling error and thus will be conservative. That is, the reported probability values will overestimate the chances of rejecting the hypothesis of no association when in fact there is an association. This bias in sampling error estimates will be counterbalanced to an unknown degree by clustering effects that arise from violating the independence assumption of traditional sampling theory.[156] Jackknifed or bootstrapped samples could provide an accurate estimate of sampling error in a cluster sample such as ours, but they would not compensate for the fact that our sample is probably a large fraction of the total population.

Our study is primarily descriptive, a "natural history" of risk professionals. Rather than attempt to develop a sampling theory appropriate to a snowball sample, we have reported the results of conventional statistical tests that assume a simple random sample from an infinite population. We have made this choice because we believe that conventional tests are an adequate, if crude, guide to the strength of associations in our data relative to sampling error.

Because this study was exploratory and descriptive, we have also relied on simple procedures, in particular Pearson's chi-square test of association in contingency tables. We chose simple analyses because the results can be understood by an audience that does not have training in multivariate analysis, and because we believe our initial examination of the risk professionals should emphasize the specifics of these individuals' characteristics and attitudes rather than the more abstract patterns that result from multivariate analysis. We suspect that more readers will be interested in the percentage of EPA employees supporting cost-benefit analysis than in the regression coefficient linking an environmental attitudes factor score to a technical policy analysis factor score.

Because we have examined a large number of contingency tables using a hypothesis testing procedure with finite statistical power, it is inevitable that we will find some statistically significant associations. We have focused our interpretation on patterns of response that persist across a number of similar variables, so our conclusions will not be artifacts of sampling error. We should also note that many of the contingency tables are "sparse," in that they have a significant fraction of cells with less than five cases, and often have highly skewed marginal distributions. The chi-square test assumes that expected frequencies are greater than five. This assumption often is violated in our analyses. Again, we note that significance levels must be interpreted with caution.

Developing the Interview Guide

Having decided whom to interview, we next had to make decisions about what to ask respondents. Most projects begin their questionnaire development by listing the topics about which information should be collected, then search through previous studies to see if sound wordings have been developed for questions that will provide the desired information. In part, we turned to previous research because we wanted to avoid reinventing the wheel. But if a study is to compare the results of two different surveys it is crucial that respondents be asked identical questions. Because we wanted to be able to compare the risk professionals with the general public, we sought to replicate previously used questions as often as possible.

For some topics of interest, question replication was not difficult. As demonstrated in Chapters 3 and 4, we were able to adopt questions from previous studies of environmental attitudes and occupational safety and health professionals. But in other cases, replication was impossible. For some issues this was because questions on risk that had been asked of the general public seemed meaningless when applied to the risk professionals. Thus, we were forced to develop a large number of new items. These went through several stages of revision. Then the purposive sample of nineteen people was interviewed with the draft interview guide. Interviewers were careful to record all respondent comments on questions and an effort was made to identify awkward sentences or questions that seemed problematic. Our respondents were encouraged to provide feedback. These pretest results identified several questions that needed changes and a few that could not be used at all. But in general we found respondent comprehension and cooperation to be excellent. To expedite the interview process, we decided to provide the respondents with copies of closed-ended questions to refer to during the interview. We then conducted a second pretest on twenty-three respondents drawn from the sampling frame using the procedures outlined above. We had no major problems with this second pretest and incorporated the data from it into the data file. A copy of the final version of the interview guide is presented verbatim in Appendix B. Copies of questions marked with an asterisk (*) were provided to the respondents to help them keep track of response categories during the interview.

Conducting the Interviews

Before conducting interviews we spent substantial time training our interviewers. Training included lectures and practice interviews with the project staff. As actual interviewing took place, completed interview guides were monitored and interviewers were periodically debriefed to check the quality of the interview data and to detect problems. In general, the interviews proceeded smoothly, but working with a highly educated and busy population proved to be more taxing than interviews with the general public, so the number of interviews conducted per day was reduced substantially from what is typical in many surveys. Altogether, six individuals, including the two principal investigators, conducted interviews. The bulk of the interviews were conducted by four graduate students at George Mason University. Some 86 percent of the total number of interviews were conducted by three of these graduate students, each of whom carried out about sixty-five interviews. This lengthened the period of time over which we collected data, but it seemed essential to provide high-quality results.

Data Coding and Data File Preparation

As soon as the interviewers returned to the project offices, they removed from the completed interview guide the cover sheet containing the respondent's name and address. These cover sheets were then placed in a locked cabinet separate from the interview guides to insure the confidentiality of the interviews.

After completion of all interviews, project staff reviewed the responses recorded for open-ended questions to develop a set of coding categories. From these categories a draft code book was prepared. Three coders, all members of the project staff who had served as interviewers, conducted the coding. As a check on the reliability of coding, a random sample of thirty interviews was drawn, and each of these was independently coded by each coder. For any item with less than a 90 percent intercoder reliability, the coding categories were reviewed and problems identified. New coding categories and more detailed decision rules were developed until all variables could be coded with adequate intercoder reliability.

Converting responses to questions into a set of categories has advantages and liabilities. The major plus, of course, is that coded data can be analyzed using a variety of statistical techniques that facilitate the discovery of patterns in the data. With 228 respondents each answering 55 questions, we had far too many data to grasp without the use of statistical techniques. But to use those techniques, we simplified the data by ignoring the rich information available in the text of our respondents' statements. To preserve this information, we also extracted quotes from the interviews. After quantitative information was completed, all recorded statements dealing with any major theme were extracted. These quotes were labeled only by the respondent's institutional affiliation and educational background to preserve confidentiality.

Not all respondents answered all questions. Nearly every respondent had difficulty interpreting some questions. But in no case was the response rate for any question so low as to preclude analysis. Nor did we find any strong patterns of nonresponse in our results, so we have chosen simply to delete those not responding to a particular question from the analysis of that item. As a consequence, the effective sample size changes slightly from question to question.

Finally, we attempted to generate some appreciation of the "quality" of the data. We asked the interviewers to categorize the quality of each interview as "good," "adequate," or "poor." While this judgment is subjective, it does provide some indication of overall data quality. Due to procedural errors, these data were not coded for five interviews, but of the remaining 223, our interviewers judged 86 percent to be of good quality, 11 percent as adequate, and only 3 percent (or seven interviews) as poor. We should also note that twenty-four interviews, or 10 percent of the total, were conducted by telephone rather than face to face.

Appendix B Interview Guide

Interviewer # _____   Sample Weight _____

Interview # _____

As the letter and previous phone call mentioned, we are conducting a study of the individuals and organizations in the U.S. environmental science and environmental policy community. The interview contains questions about your work, your background and your views. It includes both open-ended and closed-ended questions. To be able to compare our results with those of other studies we have included some questions from surveys conducted by major polling organizations. Some of these questions are very broad, but it is necessary to retain the original wording to ensure comparability. These sheets include the text of some of the closed-ended questions; they should help us get through those parts of the interview quickly. Please feel free to make any comments you care to at any point. As the letter noted, your responses will be kept strictly confidential.

THE FOLLOWING STATEMENT *MUST* BE READ TO ALL RESPONDENTS:

This interview is completely voluntary—if we come to any question which you do not want to answer, just let me know and we will go on to the next question.

1. May I proceed?
   1. Yes _____   2. No _____

2. I'd like to ask some questions about your work. What exactly is your position, and what are your duties?

   PROBE: If you had to categorize your work, would you say the majority of your time is spent in:
   _____ conducting research
   _____ supervising research
   _____ developing policy from research
   _____ translating and interpreting scientific information
   _____ or working directly on policy issues
   _____ Other (specify) _____

3. What are the largest satisfactions in your work?

4. What are the largest frustrations in your work?

5. In carrying out your work, are there any organizations, offices, groups or individuals that you talk to on a regular basis, say in a typical month?

   PROBE: In a typical month, would you have contact with:
   1. Yes _____   2. No _____ Environmental Protection Agency (IF YES: which offices?)

1. Yes _____ 2. No _____ Food and Drug Administration (IF YES: which offices?)

1. Yes _____ 2. No _____ Nuclear Regulatory Commission (IF YES: which offices?)

1. Yes _____ 2. No _____ National Institute of Environmental Health Sciences (NIEHS)

1. Yes _____ 2. No _____ Occupational Safety and Health Administration (OSHA)

1. Yes _____ 2. No _____ National Institute of Occupational Safety and Health (NIOSH)

1. Yes _____ 2. No _____ Department of Energy

1. Yes _____ 2. No _____ National Cancer Institute (NCI)

1. Yes _____ 2. No _____ Other Federal Agencies (names)

1. Yes _____ 2. No _____ Congressional Staff (IF YES: what members or committees?)

1. Yes _____ 2. No _____ Consulting Firms (IF YES: which ones?)

1. Yes _____ 2. No _____ Environmental Organizations (IF YES: which ones?)

1. Yes _____ 2. No _____ Consumer Groups (IF YES: which ones?)

1. Yes _____   2. No _____ Labor Organizations (IF YES: which ones?)

1. Yes _____   2. No _____ Industry or Trade Organizations (IF YES: which ones?)

1. Yes _____   2. No _____ Corporations (IF YES: which ones?)

6. What do you feel are the biggest problems with the environmental policy process at present?

*7. Environmental policy debates are often very heated. Several reasons have been proposed as to why such a high degree of controversy develops. We would like to know how important you feel each of the following factors is in generating public controversy about environmental policy. For each would you tell us if, in your experience, it is *a major source of controversy, a minor source of controversy,* or *not really a source of controversy?*

    A. Misunderstanding and fears on the part of the public.
        _____ 1. major source of controversy
        _____ 2. minor source of controversy
        _____ 3. not really a source of controversy
        _____ 9. D.K., N.R.

    B. An uneven distribution of net risk and benefits in which those who benefit from a situation don't bear the risks.
        _____ 1. major source of controversy
        _____ 2. minor source of controversy
        _____ 3. not really a source of controversy
        _____ 9. D.K., N.R.

    C. Differences in individual values regarding risk-taking and uncertainty.
        _____ 1. major source of controversy
        _____ 2. minor source of controversy
        _____ 3. not really a source of controversy
        _____ 9. D.K., N.R.

D. Public mistrust of government.
- _____ 1. major source of controversy
- _____ 2. minor source of controversy
- _____ 3. not really a source of controversy
- _____ 9. D.K., N.R.

E. Public mistrust of industry
- _____ 1. major source of controversy
- _____ 2. minor source of controversy
- _____ 3. not really a source of controversy
- _____ 9. D.K., N.R.

Of the five, which would you say is usually most important?
- _____ 1. A
- _____ 2. B
- _____ 3. C
- _____ 4. D
- _____ 5. E
- _____ 6. all equally important
- _____ 9. D.K., N.R.

*8. A number of ideas have been proposed to reduce the intensity of controversy involved in environmental policy debates. For each of the following ideas could you tell me if you think it would *greatly reduce controversy, reduce controversy somewhat,* or *have no effect, increase controversy somewhat,* or *greatly increase controversy*?

A. Providing the public with more accurate scientific information on environmental risks.
- _____ 1. greatly reduce
- _____ 2. reduce somewhat
- _____ 3. no effect
- _____ 4. increase somewhat
- _____ 5. greatly increase
- _____ 9. D.K., N.R.

B. Strictly control communication between industry and government.
- _____ 1. greatly reduce
- _____ 2. reduce somewhat
- _____ 3. no effect

- _____ 4. increase somewhat
- _____ 5. greatly increase
- _____ 9. D.K., N.R.

C. Provide public funding for intervenor groups, such as environmentalists, to develop their own scientific analyses to complement those of government.
- _____ 1. greatly reduce
- _____ 2. reduce somewhat
- _____ 3. no effect
- _____ 4. increase somewhat
- _____ 5. greatly increase
- _____ 9. D.K., N.R.

D. Arrange mediation or other conflict resolution procedures outside of standard legal or regulatory procedures.
- _____ 1. greatly reduce
- _____ 2. reduce somewhat
- _____ 3. no effect
- _____ 4. increase somewhat
- _____ 5. greatly increase
- _____ 9. D.K., N.R.

E. Arrange for compensation to gain support of those adversely impacted by a policy.
- _____ 1. greatly reduce
- _____ 2. reduce somewhat
- _____ 3. no effect
- _____ 4. increase somewhat
- _____ 5. greatly increase
- _____ 9. D.K., N.R.

F. Encourage political discussion to focus on value questions rather than technical issues.
- _____ 1. greatly reduce
- _____ 2. reduce somewhat
- _____ 3. no effect
- _____ 4. increase somewhat
- _____ 5. greatly increase
- _____ 9. D.K., N.R.

If you had to choose one of these as the highest priority, which would you pick?

_____ 1. A
_____ 2. B
_____ 3. C
_____ 4. D
_____ 5. E
_____ 6. F
_____ 8. none
_____ 9. D.K., N.R.

*9. How influential do you feel scientific research is in resolving policy disputes? Would you say it is *extremely influential, moderately influential, slightly influential,* or *not at all influential*?
_____ 1. extremely influential
_____ 2. moderately influential
_____ 3. slightly influential
_____ 4. not at all influential
_____ 9. D.K., N.R.

In particular, do you feel good science changes people's minds?
_____ 1. yes
_____ 2. no
_____ 3. mixed
_____ 4. D.K., N.R.

*10. In your experience, how well do policymakers understand the environmental science that underpins policy? Would you say that most policy makers have:
_____ 1. a good understanding
_____ 2. a basic understanding
_____ 3. a minimal understanding
_____ 4. don't really understand the science
_____ 9. D.K., N.R.

*11. In addition to public controversy about environmental policy, there are often disputes among experts on technical matters. The following is a list of factors that are often involved in disputes among experts in environmental science. We would like to know if you feel each of them is *almost always* involved in such technical disputes, *fre-*

quently involved in disputes, *only occasionally* involved, or *not* involved?

A. Experts "arguing past" each other by focusing on different points.
   _____ 1. almost always involved
   _____ 2. frequently involved
   _____ 3. only occasionally involved
   _____ 4. not involved
   _____ 9. D.K., N.R.

B. Ambiguities resulting in different assumptions or judgments.
   _____ 1. almost always involved
   _____ 2. frequently involved
   _____ 3. only occasionally involved
   _____ 4. not involved
   _____ 9. D.K., N.R.

C. Experts rejecting the validity of data discrepant with their position.
   _____ 1. almost always involved
   _____ 2. frequently involved
   _____ 3. only occasionally involved
   _____ 4. not involved.
   _____ 9. D.K., N.R.

D. Alternative interpretations of the same information.
   _____ 1. almost always involved
   _____ 2. frequently involved
   _____ 3. only occasionally involved
   _____ 4. not involved
   _____ 9. D.K., N.R.

E. Polarization resulting from differences in politics, paradigms, or position.
   _____ 1. almost always involved
   _____ 2. frequently involved
   _____ 3. only occasionally involved
   _____ 4. not involved
   _____ 9. D.K., N.R.

*12. As risk analysis becomes more influential in environmental policy, technical disputes may become sharper. Several proposals have been made to reduce such conflicts. For each of the following proposals, could you tell me if you feel it would be *very useful, somewhat useful, not very useful,* or *not useful at all* in resolving technical disputes.

A. Providing a code of professional practice and ethics within which experts could resolve disputes.
- _____ 1. very useful
- _____ 2. somewhat useful
- _____ 3. not very useful
- _____ 4. not useful at all
- _____ 9. D.K., N.R.

B. Having technical debates resolved through a peer review process.
- _____ 1. very useful
- _____ 2. somewhat useful
- _____ 3. not very useful
- _____ 4. not useful at all
- _____ 9. D.K., N.R.

C. Having disagreeing experts confront each other as adversaries before a panel of judges.
- _____ 1. very useful
- _____ 2. somewhat useful
- _____ 3. not very useful
- _____ 4. not useful at all
- _____ 9. D.K., N.R.

13. Recent years have seen increased use of formal techniques of analysis, such as risk analysis and benefit-cost analysis. How influential do you feel these techniques are in policymaking?

14. Do you favor or oppose the use of formal risk analysis in environmental policymaking?

15. There have been a number of proposals to standardize federal risk assessment activities in a single office or agency. How do you feel about this idea?

IF NO: Even if risk analysis were not housed in a single office, do you feel it would be a good idea to standardize procedures across agencies?

16. Do you favor or oppose government use of benefit-cost analysis in environmental policymaking?

   PROBE: why?

17. How do you feel about the use of short-term, high-dose animal studies as a basis for environmental regulation?

   PROBE: why?

18. Do you believe there are threshold levels below which most carcinogens have little or no effect?

*19. Some assert that American society is becoming overly sensitive to risk and that we now expect to be sheltered from *almost all* dangers. Others say that society is simply becoming more aware of risks and that we are now starting to take realistic precautions. Do you think that American society is becoming *overly sensitive* to risk or are we *becoming more aware of risk* and taking realistic precautions?
   _____ 1. overly sensitive to risk
   _____ 2. more aware of risk
   _____ 3. both
   _____ 9. not sure

*20. A number of economists think that ultimately one must place a value on human life, that is, decide how much money society is prepared to invest in order to prevent one additional death or save one additional life year. Do you agree or disagree that society must attempt to place an economic value on human life in order to allocate scarce resources?

_____ 1. agree
_____ 2. disagree
_____ 9. D.K., N.R.

*21. Three methods are currently being used by economists to place an economic value on human life. I would like to get your opinion of these methods.
   A. Compute the amount of earnings that would be lost in the case of premature death or disability and equate this with the value of life/disability.
   B. Ask individuals how much they would be willing to pay to reduce the probability of death or disability.
   C. Analyze wage differentials in occupations involving varying risks of injury and death and use the wage rate differentials as reflections of societal willingness to pay for decreases in risk.

   If you had to choose a technique for valuing life or injury, which technique would you select?
   _____ 1. A
   _____ 2. B
   _____ 3. C
   _____ 4. none
   _____ 9. D.K., N.R.

*22. Scholars differ about the need to consider the *distribution* of risks and benefits in formulating occupational and environmental regulation. Three dominant perspectives are:
   A. People should be allowed to make their own choices. If a worker decides to work in a risky place, he or she implicitly accepts the risks.
   B. The major rule should be that aggregate societal costs should not exceed aggregate societal benefits.
   C. Decisions should be made so that no one group bears a disproportionate share of the risks.

   Which of these is closest to your view?
   _____ 1. A
   _____ 2. B
   _____ 3. C
   _____ 4. none

The next series of questions are drawn from surveys of the general population. We are asking them to provide a base of comparison between experts and the general public.

As a general indication of your views, please tell me whether you tend to agree strongly, agree, disagree, or disagree strongly with the following statements:

*23. Society has only perceived the tip of the iceberg with regard to the risks associated with modern technology.
　　　_____ 1. AS
　　　_____ 2. A
　　　_____ 3. D
　　　_____ 4. DS
　　　_____ 9. D.K., N.R.

*24. In our democratic society, it is healthy to have an adversary relationship between business and government in areas such as product safety, pollution standards, and safety in the workplace.
　　　_____ 1. AS
　　　_____ 2. A
　　　_____ 3. D
　　　_____ 4. DS
　　　_____ 9. D.K., N.R.

*25. The balance of nature is delicate and easily upset by human activities.
　　　_____ 1. AS
　　　_____ 2. A
　　　_____ 3. D
　　　_____ 4. DS
　　　_____ 9. D.K., N.R.

*26. A high level of public involvement often leads to bad policy decisions.
　　　_____ 1. AS
　　　_____ 2. A
　　　_____ 3. D
　　　_____ 4. DS
　　　_____ 9. D.K., N.R.

*27. Scientific information is often used to justify decisions made on political grounds.
- ___ 1. AS
- ___ 2. A
- ___ 3. D
- ___ 4. DS
- ___ 9. D.K., N.R.

*28. Humanity is severely abusing the environment.
- ___ 1. AS
- ___ 2. A
- ___ 3. D
- ___ 4. DS
- ___ 9. D.K., N.R.

*29. A consumer should be allowed to choose between a very safe product at a higher price and the same product without safety equipment at a lower price.
- ___ 1. AS
- ___ 2. A
- ___ 3. D
- ___ 4. DS
- ___ 9. D.K., N.R.

*30. On the whole business does a good job of protecting the public from dangerous products and substances.
- ___ 1. AS
- ___ 2. A
- ___ 3. D
- ___ 4. DS
- ___ 9. D.K., N.R.

*31. Many environmental policy problems could be resolved with better technical information.
- ___ 1. AS
- ___ 2. A
- ___ 3. D
- ___ 4. DS
- ___ 9. D.K., N.R.

*32. The risks associated with advanced technology have been greatly exaggerated by events such as Three Mile Island or the Love Canal.
　　　____ 1. AS
　　　____ 2. A
　　　____ 3. D
　　　____ 4. DS
　　　____ 9. D.K., N.R.

*33. The government should engage in more long-range planning.
　　　____ 1. AS
　　　____ 2. A
　　　____ 3. D
　　　____ 4. DS
　　　____ 9. D.K., N.R.

*34. No substance should be permitted to be added to any food or drug if it is found to induce cancer when consumed in any dosage by humans or animals.
　　　____ 1. AS
　　　____ 2. A
　　　____ 3. D
　　　____ 4. DS
　　　____ 9. D.K., N.R.

*35. The political process treats most groups fairly.
　　　____ 1. AS
　　　____ 2. A
　　　____ 3. D
　　　____ 4. DS
　　　____ 9. D.K., N.R.

*36. Most policy decisions reflect the needs of special interest groups rather than the needs of the general public.
　　　____ 1. AS
　　　____ 2. A
　　　____ 3. D
　　　____ 4. DS
　　　____ 9. D.K., N.R.

*37. The benefits of modern consumer products are more important than the pollution caused by their production and use.
   _____ 1. AS
   _____ 2. A
   _____ 3. D
   _____ 4. DS
   _____ 9. D.K., N.R.

*38. Development of advanced technology should continue in as uninhibited a regulatory environment as reasonably possible.
   _____ 1. AS
   _____ 2. A
   _____ 3. D
   _____ 4. DS
   _____ 9. D.K., N.R.

*39. If you have a say in making up the federal budget this year, should federal spending on improving and protecting the environment be:
   _____ 1. increased
   _____ 2. kept about the same
   _____ 3. decreased
   _____ 9. D.K., N.R.

There are very many interest groups and organizations that try to influence environmental policy. We would like to get your view on each of these groups. In particular, we would like to know if you feel the group is influential and if you are sympathetic to it.

*40. First, *industry*. Would you say *industry* is very influential, somewhat influential or not influential in environmental policy making?
   _____ 1. very influential
   _____ 2. somewhat influential
   _____ 3. not influential
   _____ 9. D.K., N.R.

*41. Do you consider yourself very sympathetic, somewhat sympathetic or not sympathetic to *industry*?
　_____ 1. very sympathetic
　_____ 2. somewhat sympathetic
　_____ 3. not sympathetic
　_____ 9. D.K., N.R.

*42. Next, *the environmental movement*. Would you say the environmental movement is very influential, somewhat influential, or not influential?
　_____ 1. very influential
　_____ 2. somewhat influential
　_____ 3. not influential
　_____ 9. D.K., N.R.

*43. Do you consider yourself very sympathetic, somewhat sympathetic or not sympathetic to *the environmental movement*?
　_____ 1. very sympathetic
　_____ 2. somewhat sympathetic
　_____ 3. not sympathetic
　_____ 9. D.K., N.R.

*44. Would you say *labor unions* are very influential, somewhat influential or not influential in the environmental policy process?
　_____ 1. very influential
　_____ 2. somewhat influential
　_____ 3. not influential
　_____ 9. D.K., N.R.

*45. Do you consider yourself very sympathetic, somewhat sympathetic or not sympathetic to *labor unions*?
　_____ 1. very sympathetic
　_____ 2. somewhat sympathetic
　_____ 3. not sympathetic
　_____ 9. D.K., N.R.

46. In this study, we want to interview people whose professional activities are centered on assessing environmental

risks or debating policies intended to avert or mitigate environmental risks. We are interested in individuals in both the public and private sectors. Could you suggest five individuals we might want to interview?

	Name	Organization	Phone #
1.			
2.			
3.			
4.			
5.			

We're just about finished. I have just a few questions about your background, and a couple about politics.

47. Could you sketch your education for me, including colleges, major, and degree?

> For Undergraduate Degree:
> If answered with a University, be sure to ask which college

College	Dates	Degree	Major

Let me make sure I have your title and the name of your office correct. (IF UNCERTAIN: Is this a for-profit or a not-for-profit organization?)

48. Could you sketch your previous employment history, including where you worked, for how long, and a general idea of what your job entailed?

Employer	Dates	Job Responsibilities
_____	_____	_____
_____	_____	_____
_____	_____	_____
_____	_____	_____
_____	_____	_____

49. To what professional organizations do you belong?

50. In what year were you born?

*51. a. In your own mind, do you think of yourself as a supporter of one of the political parties, or not?
　　　_____ 1. Yes, supporter [Ask b, c, d, e]
　　　_____ 2. No, not supporter [Ask d, e]
　　　_____ 9. D.K., N.R.

　　b. IF YES ON "a": Which political party do you support?
　　　_____ 1. Republican
　　　_____ 2. Democrat
　　　_____ 3. Other (specify) _____
　　　_____ 8. INAP [No, D.K. on a]
　　　_____ 9. D.K., N.R.

　　c. IF YES ON "a": On a scale from 1 to 7, where 1 means "not very strongly" and 7 means "very strongly," please tell me the number that describes how strongly you support the party.
　　　_____ 1. Not very strongly
　　　_____ 2.
　　　_____ 3.
　　　_____ 4.
　　　_____ 5.
　　　_____ 6.
　　　_____ 7.
　　　_____ 8. INAP [No, D.K. on a]
　　　_____ 9. D.K., N.R.

d. IF YES OR NO ON "a": On a scale of 1 to 7, where 1 means feeling very close to the Republican Party and 7 means very close to the Democratic Party, where would you place yourself?
—— 1. Very close to Republican Party
—— 2.
—— 3.
—— 4.
—— 5.
—— 6.
—— 7. Very close to Democratic Party
—— 8. INAP [D.K. on a]
—— 9. [D.K., N.R.]

e. Do you ever think of yourself as a political Independent, or not?
—— 1. Yes [Ask f]
—— 2. No [Skip f]
—— 3. D.K., N.R. [Skip f]

f. IF YES ON "e": On a scale from 1 to 7 where 1 means "not very strongly Independent" and 7 means "very strongly Independent," which number describes how strongly independent in politics you feel?
—— 1. Not very strongly Independent
—— 2.
—— 3.
—— 4.
—— 5.
—— 6.
—— 7. Very strongly Independent
—— 8. INAP [No or D.K. on e]
—— 9. D.K., N.R.

*52. Finally, would you describe yourself as
—— 1. Very liberal
—— 2. Liberal
—— 3. Middle of the road
—— 4. Conservative
—— 5. Very conservative
—— 9. D.K., N.R.

53. Race:
Asian American _____
Black _____
White _____
Other _____
Can't classify _____

54. Sex of respondent: 1. Male _____
       2. Female _____

55. What is your assessment of respondent's cooperation and comprehension?

56. What questions worked well, and which failed?

Notes

¹William D. Ruckelshaus, "Science, Risk, and Public Policy," speech by the administrator of the Environmental Protection Agency to the National Academy of Sciences, Washington, DC, June 22, 1983.

²Conservation Foundation, *State of the Environment: An Assessment at Mid-Decade* (Washington, DC: Conservation Foundation, 1984); Robert W. Kates, "Success, Strain, and Surprise," *Issues in Science and Technology* 2 (Fall 1984): 46–58; and Michael Shodell, "Risky Business," *Science 85* 6 (October 1985): 43–47.

³Paul C. Stern, Thomas Dietz, and J. Stanley Black, "Support for Environmental Protection: The Role of Moral Norms," *Population and Environment* 8 (Fall-Winter 1985–86): 204–222.

⁴Anthony E. Ladd, Thomas C. Hood, and Kent D. Van Liere, "Ideological Themes in the Antinuclear Movement: Consensus and Diversity," *Sociological Inquiry* 53 (1983): 252–272; and William R. Freudenberg and Eugene A. Rosa, eds., *Public Reactions to Nuclear Power: Are There Critical Masses?* (Boulder, CO: Westview Press, 1984).

⁵Murray L. Weidenbaum, "The New Wave of Government Regulation of Business," *Business and Society Review* 15 (Fall 1975): 81–86.

⁶Paul H. Weaver, "Regulation, Social Policy, and Class Conflict," *Public Interest* 26 (Winter 1978): 45–63.

⁷W. R. Catton and Riley E. Dunlap, Jr., "A New Ecological Paradigm for Post-Exuberant Society," *American Behavioral Scientist* 24 (1980): 15–47.

⁸Stephen F. Cotgrove and Andrew Duff, "Environmentalism, Middle-Class Radicalism and Politics," *Sociological Review* 28 (1980): 333–51; and Lester Milbrath,

Environmentalists: Vanguard for a New Society (Albany: State University of New York Press, 1984).

[9] Ibid.

[10] Riley E. Dunlap, "Public Opinion: Behind the Transformation," *EPA Journal* 11 (July/August 1985): 15–17.

[11] Robert W. Crandall and Lester B. Lave, eds., *The Scientific Basis for Health and Safety Regulation* (Washington, DC: Brookings Institution, 1981); Jurgen Schmandt, "Regulation and Science," *Science, Technology and Human Values* 9 (Winter 1984): 23–28; and Jurgen Schmandt and James E. Katz, "The Scientific State: A Theory with Hypotheses," *Science, Technology and Human Values* 11 (Winter 1986): 40–52.

[12] Nicholas A. Ashford, *Benefits of Environmental, Health and Safety Regulation* (Washington, DC: Government Printing Office, 1980).

[13] Ida R. Hoos, *Systems Analysis in Public Policy: A Critique*, 2nd ed. (Berkeley: University of California Press, 1983); and George W. Downs and Patrick D. Larkey, *The Search for Government Efficiency: From Hubris to Helplessness* (New York: Random House, 1986).

[14] Guy Benveniste, *The Politics of Expertise*, 2nd ed. (San Francisco: Boyd & Fraser, 1977); Allan Mazur, *The Dynamics of Technical Controversy* (Washington, DC: Communications Press, 1981); and Allan Mazur, "Bias in Risk-Benefit Analysis," *Technology in Society* 7 (1985): 25–30.

[15] Jurgen Habermas, *Toward a Rational Society* (Boston: Beacon Press, 1970); Sanford A. Lakoff, "Scientists, Technologists and Political Power," in Ina Spiegel-Rosing and Derek de Solla Price, eds., *Science, Technology and Society: A Cross-Disciplinary Perspective* (Beverly Hills, CA: Sage Publications, 1977), pp. 355–91; Richard Sclove, "Decision-Making in a Democracy," *Bulletin of the Atomic Scientists* 38 (May 1982): 44–49; Malcolm L. Goggin, "The Life Sciences and the Public: Is Science Too Important to Be Left to the Scientists?" *Politics and the Life Sciences* 3 (August 1984): 28–40; and David Dickson, *The New Politics of Science* (New York: Pantheon, 1984).

[16] Norman J. Vig and Michael E. Kraft, "Environmental Policy from the Seventies to the Eighties," in Norman J. Vig and Michael E. Kraft, eds., *Environmental Policy in the 1980s: Reagan's New Agenda* (Washington, DC: Congressional Quarterly, 1984), pp. 3–26.

[17] See Crandall and Lave, Scientific Basis; and W. Kip Viscusi, *Risk by Choice: Regulating Health and Safety in the Workplace* (Cambridge, MA: Harvard University Press, 1983).

[18] See Don E. Kash and Robert W. Rycroft, *U.S. Energy Policy: Crisis and Complacency* (Norman: University of Oklahoma Press, 1984).

[19] See Andrew S. McFarland, *Public Interest Lobbies: Decision Making on Energy* (Washington, DC: American Enterprise Institute for Public Policy Research, 1977); and Hugh Heclo, *A Government of Strangers: Executive Politics in Washington* (Washington, DC: Brookings Institution, 1977).

[20] T. B. Bottomore, *Elites and Society* (Hammondsworth, England: Penguin Books, 1964).

[21] Irving Kristol, "Corporate Capitalism in America," *Public Interest* 37 (1975): 124–43; and Alvin W. Gouldner, *The Future of Intellectuals and the Rise of the New Class* (New York: Oxford University Press, 1979).

[22] Mazur, *The Dynamics of Technical Controversy*.

[23] David Knoke and Edward O. Laumann, "Issue Publics in National Policy Domains," paper prepared for presentation at the annual meeting of the American Sociological Association, Detroit, September 1983; and Don E. Kash and Robert W. Rycroft, "Energy Policy: How Failure Was Snatched from the Jaws of Success," *Policy Studies Review* 4 (February 1985): 433–44.

[24] Russell Sage Foundation, *Russell Sage Foundation 1980 and 1981* (New York: Russell Sage Foundation, 1982).

[25] Bottomore, *Elites and Society.*

[26] Gaetano Mosca, *The Ruling Class* (New York: McGraw-Hill, 1939); and Vilfredo Pareto, *Compendium of General Sociology* (Minneapolis: University of Minnesota Press, 1980).

[27] C. Wright Mills, *The Power Elite* (New York: Oxford University Press, 1956); and G. William Domhoff, *Who Rules America Now? A View for the 80s* (Englewood Cliffs, NJ: Prentice-Hall, 1983).

[28] Robert Dahl, *Who Governs? Democracy and Power in an American City* (New Haven, CT: Yale University Press, 1962).

[29] Mills, *The Power Elite.*

[30] Thomas Dye, *Who's Running America? The Reagan Years* (Englewood Cliffs, NJ: Prentice-Hall, 1983); Michael Useem, *The Inner Circle: Large Corporations and the Rise of Business Political Activity in the U.S. and U.K.* (New York: Oxford University Press, 1984); and Beth Mintz and Michael Swartz, *The Power Structure of American Business* (Chicago: University of Chicago Press, 1985).

[31] Roderick Nash, *Wilderness and the American Mind,* 2nd ed. (New Haven, CT: Yale University Press, 1982).

[32] Frank Graham, *Since Silent Spring* (Boston: Houghton-Mifflin, 1970).

[33] James L. Regens, Thomas M. Dietz, and Robert W. Rycroft, "Risk Assessment in the Policy-Making Process: Environmental Health and Safety Protection," *Public Administration Review* 43 (March/April 1983): 137–45.

[34] Domhoff, *Who Rules America Now?*

[35] Dye, *Who's Running America?*

[36] M. R. Hershey and P. B. Hill, "Is Pollution a 'White Thing'?: Racial Differences in Pre-Adults," *Public Opinion Quarterly* 41 (1977–78): 439–58; and Milbrath, *Environmentalists: Vanguard for a New Society.*

[37] Kent D. Van Liere and Riley E. Dunlap, "The Social Bases of Environmental Concern: A Review of Hypotheses, Explanations, and Empirical Evidence," *Public Opinion Quarterly* 44 (Summer 1980): 181–97; and Dorothy Nelkin, "Nuclear Power as a Feminist Issue," *Environment* 23 (January/February 1981): 14–20, 38–39.

[38] See John T. Bruer, "Women in Science: Toward Equitable Participation," *Science, Technology & Human Values* 9 (Summer 1984): 3–7.

[39] See Bud Ward and Jan Floyd, "Washington's Lobbying Groups: How They Rate," *Environmental Forum* 3 (April 1985); and Rochelle L. Stanfield, "Environmental Lobby's Changing of the Guard Is Part of Movement's Evolution," *National Journal* 17 (June 8, 1985): 1350–53.

[40] See Charles H. Levine, "The Federal Government in the Year 2000: Administrative Legacies of the Reagan Years," *Public Administration Review* 46 (May/June 1986): 195–206; and Bruce Adams, "The Frustrations of Government Service," *Public Administration Review* 44 (January/February 1984): 5–13.

[41] Stanfield, "Environmental Lobby's Changing of the Guard."

[42] Amitai Etzioni, "The World Class University That Our City Has Become," *Washington Post* (April 28, 1985): C1.

[43] David Foreman, "Making the Most of Professionalism," *Whole Earth Review* 45 (1985): 34–37.

[44] Steven Brint, " 'New Class' and Cumulative Trend Explanations of Liberal Political Attitudes of Professionals," *American Journal of Sociology* 90 (No. 1, 1984): 30–71; and John Ehrenreich and Barbara Ehrenreich, "The Professional-Managerial Class," *Radical America* 11 (1977): 7–31.

[45] John K. Galbraith, *The New Industrial State* (Boston: Houghton-Mifflin, 1967); Daniel Bell, *The Coming of Post-Industrial Society* (New York: Basic Books, 1973); Everett C. Ladd, Jr., "Pursuing the New Class: Social Theory and Survey Data," in B. Bruce-Briggs, ed., *The New Class?* (New Brunswick, NJ: Transaction Books, 1979), pp. 252–72; and Ladd, "The New Lines are Drawn: Class and Ideology in America," *Public Opinion Quarterly* 3 (1978): 48–53.

[46] Brint, " 'New Class' and Cumulative Trend Explanations."

[47] See Galbraith, *The New Industrial State;* and Irving Kristol, "About Equity," *Commentary* 54 (1972): 41–57.

[48] Stephen F. Cotgrove, *Catastrophe or Cornucopia: The Environment, Politics and the Future* (New York: Wiley, 1982), pp. 96–97.

[49] Catton and Dunlap, "A New Ecological Paradigm."

[50] Cotgrove and Duff, "Environmentalism, Middle-class Radicalism and Politics."

[51] Louis Harris and Associates, *Risk in a Complex Society* (New York: Louis Harris and Associates, 1982); Frances M. Lynn, "The Interplay of Science and Values in Assessing Environmental Risks," Ph.D. Dissertation, University of North Carolina School of Public Health, 1983; and Lynn, "The Interplay of Science and Values in Assessing and Regulating Environmental Risks," *Science, Technology, & Human Values* 11 (Spring 1986): 40–50.

[52] Riley E. Dunlap and Kent D. Van Liere, "The 'New Environmental Paradigm': A Proposed Measuring Instrument and Preliminary Results," *Journal of Environmental Education* 9 (Summer 1978): 10–19.

[53] Harris, *Risk in a Complex Society;* and Lynn, "The Interplay of Science and Values in Assessing and Regulating Environmental Risks."

[54] Ibid., p. 43.

[55] See Lester B. Lave, *The Strategy of Social Regulation: Decision Frameworks for Policy* (Washington, DC: Brookings Institution, 1981).

[56] Cotgrove and Duff, "Environmentalism, Middle-Class Radicalism and Politics."

[57] Van Liere and Dunlap, "The Social Bases of Environmental Concern"; and Cotgrove, *Catastrophe or Cornucopia.*

[58] Gouldner, *The Future of Intellectuals and the Rise of the New Class,* p. 48.

[59] Julie A. Honnold, "Age and Environmental Concern: Some Specification of Effects," *Journal of Environmental Education* 16 (1984): 4–9.

[60] See Milbrath, *Environmentalists: Vanguard for a New Society.*

[61] Cotgrove, *Catastrophe or Cornucopia.*

[62] Mary Douglas, *Risk Acceptability According to the Social Sciences* (New York: Russell Sage Foundation, 1985), p. 99.

[63] See Thomas Dietz, Paul C. Stern, and Robert W. Rycroft, "Why Is Everybody So Excited? The Social Construction of Conflict in the Environmental Policy System," paper presented to the 1984 Annual Meeting of the American Sociological Association, San Antonio, Texas; and Thomas Dietz and Robert W. Rycroft, "Chicken Little and Pollyanna: Perceptions of Risk in the Risk Policy System," paper presented to the 1987 Annual Meeting of the Midwest Sociological Society, Chicago.

[64] See Edith Efron, *The Apocalyptics* (New York: Simon & Schuster, 1984).

[65] See Albert J. Nichols and Richard J. Zeckhauser, "The Perils of Prudence: How Conservative Risk Assessment Distorts Regulation," *Regulation* 10 (November/December 1986): 13–24; and John F. Morrall, "A Review of the Record," *Regulation* 10 (November/December 1986): 25–34.

[66] See Sam C. Sarkesian, ed., *The Military-Industrial Complex: A Reassessment* (Beverly Hills, CA: Sage Publications, 1972); and Charles L. Cochran, ed., *Civil-Military Relations: Changing Concepts in the Seventies* (New York: Free Press, 1974).

[67] Mazur, *The Dynamics of Technical Controversy*.

[68] Foreman, "Making the Most of Professionalism."

[69] Mary Douglas and Aaron Wildavsky, "How Can We Know the Risks We Face? Why Risk Selection Is a Social Process," *Risk Analysis* 2 (1982): 49–51.

[70] Jonathan Lash, Katherine Gillman, and David Sheridan, *A Season of Spoils* (New York: Pantheon, 1984), p. 6.

[71] Joan Claybrook, *Retreat from Safety: Reagan's Attack on America's Health* (New York: Pantheon, 1984), p. 21.

[72] Steve Rayner, "Disagreeing About Risk: The Institutional Cultures of Risk Management and Planning for Future Generations," in Susan G. Hadden, ed., *Risk Analysis, Institutions, and Public Policy* (New York: Associated Faculty Press, 1984), pp. 150–69.

[73] Harold A. Linstone, *Multiple Perspectives for Decision Making: Bridging the Gap Between Analysis and Action* (New York: North-Holland, 1984).

[74] See James G. March and Herbert A. Simon, *Organizations* (New York: Wiley, 1958); Charles A. Lindblom, *The Intelligence of Democracy: Decision-Making Through Mutual Adjustment* (New York: Free Press, 1965); Graham T. Allison, *Essence of Decision* (Boston: Little, Brown, 1971); and Thomas Dietz, "Theory and Method in Social Impact Assessment," *Sociological Inquiry*, 57 (Winter 1987): 54–69.

[75] See Susan J. Tolchin and Martin Tolchin, *Dismantling America: The Rush to Deregulate* (Boston: Houghton-Mifflin, 1983); and Dickson, *The New Politics of Science*.

[76] William W. Lowrance, *Modern Science and Human Values* (New York: Oxford University Press, 1985), p. 124.

[77] Harvey Averch, *A Strategic Analysis of Science and Technology Policy* (Baltimore: Johns Hopkins University Press, 1985); and Rustum Roy and Deborah Shapley, *Lost at the Frontier: U.S. Science and Technology Policy Adrift* (Philadelphia: Institute for Scientific Information Press, 1985).

[78] Linstone, *Multiple Perspectives for Decision-Making*.

[79] Kenneth Prewitt, "Scientific Illiteracy and Democratic Theory," *Daedalus* 112 (Spring 1983): 51.

[80] See Gerald W. Cormick, "The Myth, the Reality, and the Future of Environmental Mediation," *Environment* 24 (September 1982): 14–20, 36–39.

[81] See Richard Wilson, "Risks and Their Acceptability," *Science, Technology, & Human Values* 9 (Spring 1984): 11–12; and Baruch Fischhoff, "Managing Risk Perceptions," *Issues in Science and Technology* 1 (Fall 1985): 83–96.

[82] See Dorothy Nelkin, "Public Attitudes and the Control of Research," in John M. Logsdon, ed., *The Research System in the 1980s: Public Policy Issues* (Philadelphia: Franklin Institute Press, 1982), pp. 13–23.

[83] Lynn, "The Interplay of Science and Values in Assessing and Regulating Environmental Risks."

[84] Ibid.

[85] William W. Lowrance, *Of Acceptable Risk: Science and the Determination of Safety* (Los Altos, CA: William Kaufman, 1976).

[86] U.S. Office of Technology Assessment, *Assessment of Technologies for Determining Cancer Risks from the Environment* (Washington, DC: U.S. Government Printing Office, 1981), p. 122.

[87] Walter A. Rosenbaum, *Environmental Politics and Policy* (Washington, DC: Congressional Quarterly, 1985), p. 96.

[88] Douglas and Wildavsky, "How Can We Know the Risks We Face?"

[89] Cathy Trost, *Elements of Risk: The Chemical Industry and Its Threats to America* (New York: Times Books, 1984); Dorothy Nelkin and Michael S. Brown, *Workers at Risk: Voices from the Workplace* (Chicago: University of Chicago Press, 1984); and Pascal J. Imperato and Greg Mitchell, *Acceptable Risks* (New York: Viking Press, 1985).

[90] Lynn, "The Interplay of Science and Values in Assessing and Regulating Environmental Risks."

[91] Viscusi, *Risk by Choice*.

[92] Lynn, "The Interplay of Science and Values in Assessing and Regulating Environmental Risks."

[93] John Chubb, *Interest Groups and the Bureaucracy: The Politics of Energy* (Stanford, CA: Stanford University Press, 1983).

[94] Mazur, "Bias in Risk-Benefit Analysis."

[95] Hoos, *Systems Analysis in Public Policy*.

[96] Kash and Rycroft, *U.S. Energy Policy*, p. 86.

[97] Charles Peters, *How Washington Really Works*, 3rd ed. (Reading, MA: Addison-Wesley, 1984).

[98] Jessica Lipnak and Jeffrey Stamps, *Networking: The First Report and Directory* (New York: Doubleday, 1982), p. 1.

[99] Stuart Langton, "Networking and the Environmental Movement," in Stuart Langton, ed., *Environmental Leadership* (Lexington, MA: D. C. Heath, 1984), p. 129.

[100] See Seymour Saranson, Charles Carol, Kenneth Maton, Saul Cohen, and Elizabeth Lorentz, *Human Services and Resource Networks* (San Francisco: Jossey-Bass, 1977).

[101] Langton, "Networking and the Environmental Movement," pp. 129–130.

[102] John W. Kingdon, *Agendas, Alternatives, and Public Policies* (Boston: Little, Brown, 1984), p. 209.

[103] Knoke and Laumann, "Issue Publics in National Policy Domains."

[104] Ibid., pp. 3–4.

[105] Ibid.; and Edward O. Laumann, David Knoke, and Hong-Hak Kim, "An Organizational Approach to State Policy Formation: A Comparative Study of Energy and Health Domains," *American Sociological Review* 50 (February 1985): 1–19.

[106] Richard J. Stillman III, *Public Administration: Concepts and Cases*, 3rd ed. (Boston: Houghton-Mifflin, 1983).

[107] Rosenbaum, *Environmental Politics and Policy*; and Stanfield, "Environmental Lobby's Changing of the Guard."

[108] Sylvia D. Fries, "Expertise Against Politics: Technology as Ideology on Capitol Hill, 1966–1972," *Science, Technology, & Human Values* 8 (Spring 1983): 6–15.

[109] George E. Brown, Jr., "Response," in Shapley and Roy, *Lost at the Frontier*, p. 168.

[110] See Aaron Wildavsky, "Wealthier Is Healthier," *Regulation* 4 (January/February 1980): 10–12; and Chris Whipple, "Redistributing Risk," *Regulation* 9 (May/June 1985): 37–44.

[111] Kash and Rycroft, *U.S. Energy Policy*; and Harry C. Kenski and Helen M. Ingram, "The Reagan Administration and Environmental Regulation: The Constraint of the Political Market," in Sheldon Kamieniecki, Robert O'Brien, and Michael Clarke, eds., *Controversies in Environmental Policy* (Albany: State University of New York Press, 1986), pp. 275–299.

[112] Harry C. Kenski and Margaret C. Kenski, "Congress Against the President: The Struggle over the Environment," in Norman J. Vig and Michael E. Kraft, eds., *Environmental Policy in the 1980s: Reagan's New Agenda* (Washington, DC: Congressional Quarterly, 1984), pp. 97–120.

[113] James L. Regens and Robert W. Rycroft, "Outlook for Intergovernmental Science and Technology: Partnership or Manipulation?" *American Review of Public Administration*, in press.

[114] Dean E. Mann, "Introduction," in Dean E. Mann, ed., *Environmental Policy Implementation* (Lexington, MA: D. C. Heath, 1982), pp. 1–34.

[115] David Knoke and James H. Kuklinski, *Network Analysis* (Beverly Hills, CA: Sage Publications, 1982); and Mark S. Aldendorfer and Roger K. Blashfield, *Cluster Analysis* (Beverly Hills, CA: Sage Publications, 1984).

[116] Kingdon, *Agendas, Alternatives, and Public Policies*.

[117] Alfred Marcus, "Environmental Protection Agency," in James Q. Wilson, ed., *The Politics of Regulation* (New York: Basic Books, 1980), pp. 267–303.

[118] Steven A. Cohen, "EPA: A Qualified Success," in Sheldon Kamieniecki, Robert O'Brien, and Michael Clarke, eds., *Controversies in Environmental Policy* (Albany: State University of New York Press, 1986), pp. 179–98.

[119] Kingdon, *Agendas, Alternatives, and Public Policies*.

[120] Stanfield, "Environmental Lobby's Changing of the Guard."

[121] Alan Schnaiberg, *The Environment: From Surplus to Scarcity* (New York: Oxford University Press, 1980); Jurgen Habermas, "The Dialectics of Rationalization," *Telos* 49 (Fall 1981): 5–31; and Claus Offe, *Contradictions of the Welfare State* (Cambridge, MA: MIT Press, 1984).

[122] See Seymour M. Lipset, "The Social Requisites of Democracy: Economic Development and Political Legitimacy," in Charles F. Cnudde and Deane E. Neubauer, eds., *Empirical Democratic Theory* (Chicago: Markham, 1969), pp. 151–92.

[123] Roger G. Noll and Bruce E. Owen, "The Predictability of Interest Group Arguments," in Roger G. Noll and Bruce M. Owens, eds., *The Political Economy of Deregulation* (Washington, DC: American Enterprise Institute for Public Policy Research, 1983), pp. 53–65.

[124] Lash, Gillman, and Sheridan, *A Season of Spoils*.

[125] Nelkin and Brown, *Workers at Risk*.

[126] Knoke and Laumann, "Issue Publics in National Policy Domains."

[127] Robert C. Mitchell, "Public Opinion and Environmental Politics in the 1970s and 1980s," in Norman J. Vig and Michael E. Kraft, eds., *Environmental Policy in the 1980s: Reagan's New Agenda* (Washington, DC: Congressional Quarterly, 1984), p. 186.

[128] James F. Short, Jr., "The Social Fabric at Risk: Toward the Social Transformation of Risk Analysis," *American Sociological Review* 49 (1984), p. 712.

[129] Dunlap, "Public Opinion: Behind the Transformation."

[130] Jack C. Plano and Milton Greenberg, *The American Political Dictionary*, 7th ed. (New York: Holt, Rinehart & Winston, 1985), p. 497.

[131] Hoos, *Systems Analysis in Public Policy*.

[132] Henry S. Kariel, *Open Systems: Arenas for Social Action* (Itasca, IL: F. E. Peacock Publishers, 1968).

[133] Hugh Heclo, "Issue Networks and the Executive Establishment," in Anthony King, ed., *The New American Political System* (Washington, DC: American Enterprise Institute for Public Policy Research, 1978), pp. 95–98.

[134] Peter Weingart, "The Scientific Elite—A Chimera: The Deinstitutionalization and Politicization of Science," in Norbert Elias, Hermino Martins, and Richard Whitley, eds., *Scientific Establishments and Hierarchies* (Boston: D. Reidel Publishing Co., 1982), p. 78.

[135] William Sweet, "Closing the Environmental Decade," in Editorial Research Reports, *Environmental Issues: Prospects and Problems* (Washington, DC: Congressional Quarterly, 1982), pp. 139–56.

[136] Stuart Langton, "The Future of the Environmental Movement," in Stuart Langton, ed., *Environmental Leadership* (Lexington, MA: D. C. Heath, 1984), pp. 5–10.

[137] Stanfield, "Environmental Lobby's Changing of the Guard."

[138] Foreman, "Making the Most of Professionalism."

[139] See issues of *Not Man Apart*, the FOE journal, between January and June, 1986.

[140] Wesley Schrum, "Scientific Specialties and Technical Systems," *Social Studies of Science* 14 (1984): 81.

[141] See Averch, *A Strategic Analysis of Science and Technology Policy*.

[142] See Dickson, *The New Politics of Science*.

[143] Schnaiberg, *The Environment: From Surplus to Scarcity*.

[144] Paul R. Ehrlich, *The Machinery of Nature* (New York: Simon & Schuster, 1986).

[145] Alvin M. Weinberg, "Science and Trans-Science," *Minerva* 10 (1972): 209–222.

[146] Karen Knorr-Cetina, *The Manufacture of Knowledge: An Essay on the Constructivist and Contextual Nature of Science* (New York: Pergamon, 1981), pp. 82–83.

[147] James Q. Wilson, "The Politics of Regulation," in James Q. Wilson, ed., *The Politics of Regulation* (New York: Basic Books, 1980), p. 393.

[148] W. R. Catton and Riley E. Dunlap, Jr., "Environmental Sociology: A New Paradigm," *American Sociologist* 13 (1978): 41–49.

[149] See Kash and Rycroft, "Energy Policy: How Failure Was Snatched from the Jaws of Success."

[150] Charles Perrow, *Normal Accidents* (New York: Basic Books, 1984).

[151] Dale Hattis and David Kennedy, "Assessing Risks from Health Hazards: An Imperfect Science," *Technology Review* 89 (May/June 1986): 62.

[152] Downs and Larkey, *The Search for Government Efficiency*.

[153] Dietz, "Theory and Method in Social Impact Assessment."

[154] Allan R. Talbot, *Settling Things: Six Studies in Environmental Mediation* (Washington, DC: Conservation Foundation, 1983).

[155] P. Holgate, "Species Frequency Distributions," *Biometrika* 56 (1969): 651–60; Donald R. McNeal, "Estimating an Author's Vocabulary," *Journal of the American Statistical Association* 68 (1973): 92–96; and Bradley Efron and Ronald Thisted, "Estimating the Number of Unknown Species: How Many Words Did Shakespeare Know?" *Biometrika* 63 (1976): 435–47.

[156] Seymour Sudman, *Applied Sampling* (New York: Academic Press, 1976).